The Modern Nations in
Historical Perspective

ROBIN W. WINKS, *General Editor*

The volumes in this series deal with individual nations or groups of closely related nations throughout the world, summarizing the chief historical trends and influences that have contributed to each nation's present-day character, problems, and behavior. Recent data are incorporated with established historical background to achieve a fresh synthesis and original interpretation.

CHARLES E. NOWELL, *author of this book, is a retired Professor of History of the University of Illinois. He is the author of numerous books, including* The History of Portugal, The Great Discoveries, Magellan's Voyage around the World, *and* A Letter to Ferdinand and Isabella.

ALSO IN THE EUROPEAN SUBSERIES

The Balkans *by Charles and Barbara Jelavich*
France *by John C. Cairnes*
Germany *by Ernest K. Bramsted*
Ireland *by Oliver MacDonagh*
Italy *by Massimo Salvadori*
Poland and Czechoslovakia *by Frederick G. Heymann*
Russia *by Robert V. Daniels*
Scandinavia *by John H. Wuorinen*
Spain *by Richard Herr*

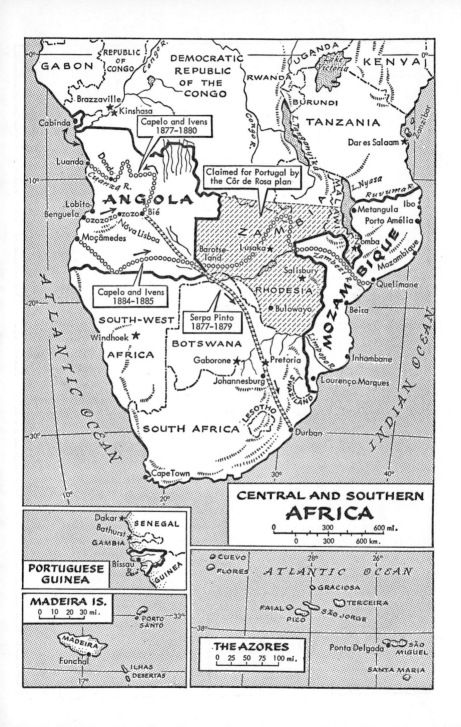

REPUBLIC OF CONGO

GABON

Congo R.

Brazzaville
Kinshasa ★

Cabinda ●

DEMOCRATIC
REPUBLIC
OF
THE
CONGO

Capelo and Ivens
1877–1880

Luanda ●

Dondo

Cuanza R.

ANGOLA

Lobito ●
Benguela ●
ozozozo zozo
Nóva Lisboa

Bié ●

Moçâmedes ●

Claimed for Portugal by
the Côr de Rosa plan

Barotse-
land

ZAMBIA

Lusaka ★

Capelo and Ivens
1884–1885

SOUTH-WEST

Windhoek ★

AFRICA

BOTSWANA

Gaborone ★

Johannesburg ●

Serpa Pinto
1877–1879

Salisbury ★

RHODESIA

Bulowayo ●

Pretoria ●

LESOTHO

SOUTH AFRICA

Durban ●

CapeTown ●

RWANDA

UGANDA

BURUNDI

Lake
Victoria

KENYA

L. Tanganyika

TANZANIA

Dar es Salaam ★

MALAWI

L. Nyasa

Ruvuma R.

Ibo ●

Metangula ●
Porto Amélia ●

Zomba ●

Mozambique ●

MOZAMBIQUE

Zambezi R.

Quelimane ●

Beira ●

Limpopo R.

SWAZILAND

Inhambane ●

Lourenço Marques ●

ATLANTIC OCEAN

INDIAN OCEAN

Zanzibar

CENTRAL AND SOUTHERN
AFRICA

0   300   600 mi.
0   300   600 km.

Dakar ★
Bathurst ★
GAMBIA
Bissau ●

SENEGAL

GUINEA

PORTUGUESE
GUINEA

MADEIRA IS.
0 10 20 30 mi.

MADEIRA

Funchal ●

PORTO
SANTO

ILHAS
DESERTAS

CUEVO ○
FLORES ○

GRACIOSA ○

FAIAL ○
PICO ○

SÃO JORGE
TERCEIRA ○

ATLANTIC OCEAN

SÃO
MIGUEL ○

Ponta Delgada ●

THE AZORES
0 25 50 75 100 mi.

SANTA MARIA

PORTUGAL

Charles E. Nowell

PRENTICE-HALL, INC. Englewood Cliffs, New Jersey

Library of Congress Cataloging in Publication Data

NOWELL, CHARLES E
    Portugal.

    (The Modern nations in historical perspective) (A
Spectrum Book)
    Bibliography: p.
    1. Portugal—History. I. Title.
DP539.N68   946.9   73–178768
ISBN 0–13–686915–7
ISBN 0–13–686907–6 (pbk)

10   9   8   7   6   5   4   3   2   1

PRENTICE-HALL INTERNATIONAL, INC. (London)
PRENTICE-HALL OF AUSTRALIA PTY. LTD. (Sydney)
PRENTICE-HALL OF CANADA LTD. (Toronto)
PRENTICE-HALL OF INDIA PRIVATE LIMITED (New Delhi)
PRENTICE-HALL OF JAPAN, INC. (Tokyo)

Contents

Preface

This survey of Portugal is partly contemporary and partly historical, with the historical emphasis placed largely on the last two centuries. There are many works offering detailed coverage of earlier
Portuguese times, and some are listed in the bibliography at the end
of the book, but those times are the ones most studied by historians
and can be given briefer treatment here. The country's political greatness has passed, but its recent history contains much that is interesting and instructive. The Portuguese ship of state has had rough
sailing in these later years; the nation has been invaded, fought civil
wars, tried every modern form of government except communism,
and struggled with problems of poverty, illiteracy, debt, inflation,
growing urbanization, and colonialism. Though it has suffered territorial losses overseas, it retains a considerable empire and is the sole
remaining old-style colonial power.

In a book as short as this, intended for nonspecialists, there must
be many generalizations—statements that are mainly true but to
which some exceptions can be cited. There are no apologies for the
generalizations, only the reminder that nothing can be said that precisely fits all situations, issues, and people.

When Portugal overthrew its monarchy and became a republic
in 1910, it made changes in national symbols, currency, and coinage.

With these came alterations in the spelling of the language, making it more phonetic and eliminating superfluous letters. The changes came not all at once but in several revisions over a period of years and naturally proved confusing to many who were obliged to relearn orthography repeatedly during their lives. Brazil, the huge daughter republic, early conformed in general to Portuguese practices and finally officially adopted them, although minor variations still exist between the spellings of the two countries. Portuguese books printed as late as 1910 contain some words spelled differently from the present forms, and although the changes made no difference in pronunciation, foreigners, unaware of the reasons for the alterations, sometimes find them puzzling. All spellings of Portuguese words used here conform to present standards except in a few cases of individuals, who may use old or new forms for their names as they please.

The biographical dates often provided here refer to the length of their lives for private individuals and to the years of their reigns for sovereigns.

Theodore Calvin Pease, 1887–1948
Salute to a soldier

1

Contemporary Portugal

Four centuries ago, Portugal, small and generally backward today, was one of the leading nations of the world. Its citizens, even though many are poorly educated, know that their country was once great among nations and spread its influence far and wide over the globe. They are aware that their kings, seamen, and captains created the first modern overseas empire, part of which still endures, but many of them realize that the past is responsible in great measure for what is wrong with the country today.

Over 100 million people today speak the Portuguese language and to some extent regard the little European state as a motherland, despite the fact that Portugal, in the past, made nearly every mistake possible for a nation. It once persecuted or expelled many of its ablest people for reasons of both religion and sheer prejudice. It adopted disastrous economic policies, though such policies were not confined to Portugal. When much of the rest of Europe was cultivating new scientific and intellectual fields, Portugal adopted a retrogressive policy and regarded such changes as dangerous. The results were severely crippling to national development.

Finally, it can be argued that the very policies that actually made it a world power were the greatest mistakes of all. The country's phenomenal rise to greatness took place in the fifteenth and sixteenth centuries, when it built a seemingly rich and enviable empire. But the price proved a heavy one; world dominion was accomplished at the cost of home development, and the little country began to stagnate even while imperialism went on. Expansion cost men—the most vigorous blood Portugal had—and proved to be a strain on the scanty national resources. Thus it exhausted itself while still young, and never regained real strength. The time came when Portugal lost independence for a period of sixty years, and although it ultimately emerged from captivity, things were never the same. The European and world situation had changed, and Portugal could not recover its former role. It continued for a time to play some part in European affairs, but this constantly lessened until, by the early nineteenth century, it had become a pawn in the rivalries of greater powers. This state of affairs has continued to an extent ever since.

Portugal has never been a democracy. From its beginnings until 1822 it was in theory an absolute monarchy, and from then until 1910 a limited monarchy. In the sixteen years after 1910 it played at being a republic with a conspicuous lack of success. Articulate public opinion was manipulated by political leaders and an often irresponsible press. When continuance of the republican experiment seemed impossible, its place was taken by a twentieth-century absolutism, influenced by fascistic ideas current at the time but with differences. For approximately forty years, the nation lived under the regime of Dr. António de Oliveira Salazar, a dictator who did not closely resemble any of his European contemporaries. He helped create present-day Portugal and governed it until incapacitated in 1968 by a stroke, which preceded his death by two years. Following the stroke, a new dictator, Dr. Marcello Caetano, governed the country somewhat more liberally.

The Portuguese are an attractive people, intelligent and industrious, living in a beautiful country. Their history, even with its mistakes, is intrinsically interesting and certainly has valuable lessons to teach. Anyone genuinely interested in the human past can often learn more from the record of a small country than of a large one.

The Country

Portugal, with an area of 35,000 square miles and a population of slightly under 10 million, is divided into eleven mainland provinces. These mean little for political purposes because the government is extremely unitary and the provinces exist for administrative convenience, though their existence perpetuates historical subdivisions important in the nation's past. The Azores and Madeira Islands, unpopulated before their colonization by Portuguese in the fifteenth century, are classed and governed as part of the nation, and their inhabitants have the same status as those on the mainland.

Portugal is rather mountainous, with the Trás-os-Montes in the northeast and the Serra da Estrêla inland between the Mondego and Tagus Rivers being the most elevated areas. Neither range rises to great heights and no peak in Portugal is as much as 7,000 feet above sea level.

Rainfall varies greatly from the wet north to the comparatively dry south. It has occasionally amounted to 16 feet per year and at such times floods have caused heavy damage and suffering. Normal rainfall, however, ranges between some 80 inches annually in the north to approximately a third of that in the extreme southern Algarve province. The difference is seen in the vegetation and color of the landscape, the northern parts being green and lush and the Algarve often described as a steppe.

Portugal has the reputation of being a poor country, and this is borne out by the condition of most of its people, in spite of the Mediterranean climate, beneficial for growing wine grapes, and the coasts, which are good for fishing. The subsoil is poor in minerals, though it yields some wolfram, tin, pyrite, coal, and uranium. About half the land is available for cultivation, slightly over 25 percent is forested, and somewhat less than 25 percent is noncultivable by present standards. The farms produce less than they might because the tillers are generally the least educated and skilled portion of the population. The minute size of most holdings makes impossible the employment of agricultural machinery, and the large estate owners, who could use tractors and harvesters, seldom do so because of the availability of cheap hand labor. The principal crops are wheat, maize, oats, barley, and, of course, wine grapes, which grow best in the north and in Madeira. Portugal is the world's leading producer of cork, which comes from the outer bark of an evergreen oak.

The country's industries are minor, with the possible exception of fast-growing tourism. The major products are textiles, glassware, artistic pottery, and paper. Heavy industry has made a start, though a slow one; the government's unyielding policy of tariff protection makes difficult the acquisition of necessary machinery. Even in supplying munitions to its limited armed forces, Portugal depends on imports from abroad. The forces consist of a few small warships, a number of up-to-date planes of foreign make, and an army of about 150,000 officers and men, to which all citizens of suitable age are liable for service. Lack of financial resources prevents the conscription of most of those available.

Fishing may also be classified as a Portuguese industry. Most salt-water fishing is near the shores and nets are even set out and hauled in from the beaches, but every year a "banker" fleet of small craft goes to the Newfoundland coasts for the *bacalhau* (cod) that is a luxury article of diet in Portugal.

Nearly half the Portuguese are at present classified as city dwellers, but this is misleading if one thinks of the vast metropolitan centers of western Europe and the United States. Except for Lisbon and Oporto, the cities of Portugal are not very large and many of their inhabitants are but one generation removed from the soil. Lisbon, in addition to being the principal city and capital, is also the country's major seaport. Next is Porto de Leixões, an artificial harbor serving the city of Oporto, whose former harbor is no longer usable for ocean vessels because of a bar that impedes navigation.

THE CAPITAL

Nature seems almost to have intended Lisbon to be the capital of Portugal. The city, situated on the north bank of the Tagus, about ten miles from its mouth, possesses a natural harbor that has no superior. Lisbon rises sharply from the river's edge, but insufficiently to impede seriously any pedestrian or vehicular traffic. The panorama one sees from many parts of the city is magnificent, and from the river Lisbon looks impressive both by day and by night.

Lisbon, with an estimated population of 828,000 today, is described as having an unkempt, run-down appearance in the 1890s. Many streets were unpaved; dusty, odoriferous rubbish heaps lay in abundance, and public transportation consisted of omnibuses drawn by puffing mules that had to be frequently halted for rests. The royal family lived as little as possible in its Necessidades Palace in the city and preferred the palace at Sintra twenty miles away, to which the most convenient access was by horseback or carriage. By the opening decade of this century, the reigning king, Carlos, and his family often resided at suburban Queluz.

Lisbon presents a very different aspect today. It is sometimes described as owing its present form to the Marquis of Pombal, who supervised the rebuilding after its partial destruction by the earthquake and tidal wave of 1755, and was responsible for the central streets, avenues, and squares, but today's city is mostly the creation of the twentieth century and especially of the Salazar regime. At present, the Lisboetas take justifiable pride in the city's appearance and cooperate to keep it clean and attractive. This care extends to the surrounding region as well. Sintra Palace is a national showplace, connected by electric train and highway with Lisbon, and the beautiful grounds around it, now a public park, are tended as one suspects they never were in monarchical times.

The heart of Lisbon is Rossio Square, quiet but by no means sleepy, on which face the central railroad station and several important public buildings. Rossio in the past has been the scene of riots and political demonstrations, but these ceased altogether soon after Salazar came to power.

The Jerónimos Church is Portugal's Westminster Abbey, in which are some of the country's most famous dead. Because the idea of a national pantheon occurred rather late, most of those in repose are nineteenth- and twentieth-century notables, including liberals that the conservative and strongly Catholic Salazar regime might not have honored thus had it been in power when they died. Portugal's two greatest heroes, the voyager Vasco da Gama and the poet Camões, are there by proxy. When it was planned to inter them in the Jerónimos in 1880, the grave of Camões in a Lisbon potter's field could not be identified, so an anonymous cadaver, unearthed at random, was substituted. Recent political disturbances at Vidigueira, the Gama country seat, and damage to the family crypt caused the famous Vasco's remains to be confused with those of a later Gama nonentity who was transported in state to the Jerónimos to the accompaniment of martial reviews and military bands.

Visible to all who sail along the Tagus or traverse its shores by Belem is the tower, beautiful in its simplicity, built by order of King Manuel I in honor of Vasco da Gama's historic voyage to India and return. As a type of architecture, it is hard to identify precisely, but the theme is evidently African.

The oldest portion of Lisbon is the Alfama, situated in the eastern part of the city near the waterfront. This dates from Roman and Moorish times, and is on hilly ground traversed by winding streets and alleys. Here live the poorer Lisbon citizens, crowded into narrow spaces and raising, as a rule, large families. There are several churches of renown and antiquity in the Alfama district, including twelfth-century São Vicente de Fora (originally "St. Vincent outside the city") and the sixteenth-century chapel of Nossa Senhora da Graça, where lie the remains of the conqueror Afonso de Albuquerque.

Lisbon beggary is by no means confined to the Alfama, though many of the mendicants live there. The law prohibits both begging and going barefoot, though there is plenty of both. Some of the beggars are undeniably needy, but others are professionals who contrive to look and dress the part. They may be engaged in gay conversation with friends, but when an easily identifiable foreigner approaches, the look changes to one of utter misery, hands are outstretched, and words mumbled, signifying poverty and need. Those who go barefoot are apt to be the genuine poor, who do have shoes but wish to save wear on them. They often carry cheap slippers which they hastily don when they spy an officer of the law.

Two fairly recent innovations in Lisbon are the subway system and the spectacular Salazar Bridge, over the Tagus, from which trains run to Évora, Beja, and the Algarve and connect the city with Barreiro, on the south bank. In 1966, at an estimated cost of $75,000,000, the great bridge was completed. It is the longest suspension bridge in Europe and was built largely by the U.S. Steel Corporation with assists from two French banks. The new structure considerably reduces travelling time to the south and has made possible an extension of the Lisbon suburban area. Yet Portuguese economists have not been altogether happy about the Salazar Bridge and say that the great sum its construction required could have been better spent on more important things.

TRANSPORTATION

Portugal has all forms of modern transportation for both internal travel and travel to and from abroad. Lisbon has an excellent airport and Oporto a somewhat smaller one, the capital being served by most of the world's major airlines. The country's own passenger line, *Transportes Aéreos Portugueses* (TAP), connects Lisbon with western European countries, the Portuguese Atlantic islands, Brazil, and Portuguese Africa.

The excellent and modern Lisbon harbor is a port of call for numerous passenger and freight lines. Passenger steamship service has declined the world over because of air competition, but one may still sail from Lisbon to France, England, and South America.

Portuguese passenger trains are clean and well run, better than those of Spain or most of the few remaining ones in the United States. Most of the railroads were built by the British in the nineteenth century; steam appears to be altogether replaced by electric and diesel engines.

Partly to accommodate the growing number of tourists who have "discovered" Portugal since World War II, a good network of highways now connects the major points of the country. The Algarve, a southern province with a strong Moorish background that makes it almost a part of Africa, has especially sought to take advantage of *turismo* by building new hotels and *pousadas* (inns or auto cabins). Northern Portugal is cold in winter, but in the south tourism can be a year-round industry. The south may be said to include the Madeira Islands, which were the first part of Portugal to attract numbers of winter visitors.

Tourism furnishes employment to many in addition to those in the food and lodging business; the transportation, building, artistic, and agricultural occupations all have a share. The central association of tourism in Portugal estimates that the main influx of sightseeing foreigners is yet to come, and has established schools for training knowledgeable employees, and hotel schools similar to those of Denmark.

RELIGION

Nearly all the Portuguese are Roman Catholic, a statement that may be qualified by the reminder that everyone is so classified who does not profess to be anything else. A few thousand declare themselves atheists or agnostics, and Portugal is tolerant enough to permit them to do so. The Roman religion is not an avowed established faith and worship is announced as free. But although there is no state church in Portugal, Catholicism is so overwhelmingly the belief of the people that the government takes particular notice of it and gives it special attention. Religious toleration in Portugal allows Protestants, mostly foreigners, to have places of worship and practice their religion, but it is considered good form for them to do so with a minimum of ostentation. The ancient alliance between Portugal and Great Britain allows for an important exception: the Anglican church in Lisbon is spacious and has its own burial grounds. English clergymen perform services in their own language, though many of those attending appear to be Portuguese. There are a few other Protestant churches in Lisbon and a Jewish synagogue, but these are inconspicuous.

Portugal has two cardinals, one of whom is the Patriarch of Lisbon and the other, theoretically his equal, is without a precise territorial jurisdiction. The northern city of Braga, small today and otherwise of minor importance, is the oldest see in Portugal and enjoys special prestige on that account. The shrine of Fátima, even though named for a daughter of Mohammed, is important to the devout because of miracles reported there in 1917. Between May and October of that year, the Virgin Mary is supposed to have appeared six times to three children, Lucia de Jesús, age ten, and Francisco and Jacinta Martó, both somewhat younger. She urged repentance of sins and recitation of the rosary by the whole world. The Virgin also asked that all countries, and in particular Russia, be consecrated to her Sacred Heart. At the last apparition, on a dark rainy day, the children said they saw the sun suddenly shine and tremble in the sky, moving considerably before returning to its former place. There were by this time many spectators watching, and some of them declared that they saw the same phenomenon beheld by little Maria, though the Virgin did not reveal herself to them, nor was the unusual solar motion visible at any other place. The church authorities, and at last the papacy, approved devotion to Our Lady of Fátima, and a basilica built there in 1944 is visited daily by pilgrims from Portugal and abroad.

Portuguese Catholicism has been called ignorant and superstitious, and it would have been difficult to refute this charge a century or less ago. The nineteenth-century novelist, José Maria Eça de Queirós, in The Relic, The Crime of Father Amaro, and Maias, in which the clergy as a rule are pictured as greedy and sensual, may have exaggerated as well in his portrayal of the superstitious ignorance of the Portuguese woman, but he was nonetheless describing a society he knew very well.

In the years after 1910, under the early republic, the Church in Portugal was not only disestablished but underwent persecution, because the republican leaders were largely positivists, freemasons, or atheists. One good result came of this, however, because priests who had taken orders simply for the prestige and easy living they might enjoy left the Church, which was thereafter in the hands of fewer but more genuinely devout clergymen. It is safe to say that Portugal practices a more intelligent brand of Catholicism today, though remains of the old are still seen.

Some call the Portuguese the most Catholic people in the world. The fact is not particularly noticeable to foreign observers, but these customarily see more of city than country life. Rural Portuguese are certainly more devout than those in the urban centers, though peasants in the past have been known to go on rampages and burn religious edifices, showing themselves, temporarily at least, anticlerical if not anti-Catholic.

Portuguese priests and nuns are less in evidence than their Spanish counterparts, and the former dress for street purposes as do those of the United States; in black with clerical collars but without the cassock. This is in contrast to the Spanish clergy, who wear the long robe everywhere.

EDUCATION, THE PRESS, AND LITERATURE

Portugal has five universities, of which the oldest and most famous is Coimbra, founded at Lisbon in 1290, later moved back and forth between there and Coimbra, and permanently situated at Coimbra since 1527. Throughout most of Portuguese history it has been the only university, and the majority of the country's literary greats, statesmen, and professional people have completed their educations there. It has been fashionable in the twentieth century to sneer at Coimbra and call it the best medieval university in the world. Although this was somewhat true in the not-too-distant past, it does not altogether apply at present; Coimbra teaches the sciences, up-to-date medicine, and the principal modern languages and literatures. What may be said on the unfavorable side is that its faculty, government appointees, must conform to the views of the regime, and on this account there have been so many dismissals and resignations that most of Portugal's most distinguished scientists and scholars are not found there.

Coimbra, long a masculine stronghold, has become coeducational. Salazar once admitted that although he had no great personal interest in female emancipation he felt powerless to stop it. Students wear black gowns, shorter than the academic robes known in the United States. They are not traditionally a passive group and have been known to riot and boycott classes in support of causes, usually liberal or radical. Next to Coimbra, the most important universities are those of Lisbon and Oporto; and in addition Portugal has numerous polytechnical schools, several colleges of art and music, and military and naval academies.

Until well into the twentieth century, the writers of Portugal addressed a rather small reading public. When the monarchy expired in 1910, the country had 5 million people, of whom an estimated 60 percent were illiterate. Well-known authors had additional readers in Brazil, with a much larger population but also a low literacy rate. The early republic and the Salazar regime made some strides in correcting the bad situation, but the small national budget and the poverty of many areas has not permitted an adequate system of public schools. By a recent estimate, about 70 percent of Portuguese males and a somewhat lower percentage of females are classed as able to read and write. This raises the perplexing question of a correct definition of literacy. For some, certainly, it means the ability to make out simple words and to write one's name, but hardly the competence to read books or understand much of the daily press. Even allowing this, the percentage of *analfabetos* (illiterates) has been substantially, though insufficiently, reduced in two generations.

Before the dictatorship, the Portuguese press tended to be unbridled and irresponsible. It took violent sides in every controversy; it raged and stormed and hurled insults and often preposterous accusations at those with different views. Under Salazar, the newspapers, of which the Lisbon *Diário de Notícias*, the nation's leading daily, is a prime example, became very dull reading by contrast. All was serenity and contentment; there was little national political news except of a routine nature, such as the appointment of a new official or the ceremonious reception of a foreign ambassador. Hospitals and orphanages received full coverage, as did schools and religious societies and wheat production figures from the Alentejo or the Algarve. Foreign political news consisted of releases from outside press agencies translated into Portuguese. English and American readers would have found most of this rather dreary fare, and to all appearances the Portuguese found it the same. Foreign journals and magazines, however, could be purchased at some newsstands and seemed to command a ready sale; with occasional exceptions, there was no attempt to restrict or censor them. Under Caetano, somewhat more latitude was permitted the Portuguese press, which was allowed, and to some extent encouraged, to criticize the government.

Portugal has produced many good writers in the twentieth century, but thus far no towering literary figures to match the galaxy of the nineteenth that included Almeida Garrett, Herculano, Eça de Queirós, and Antero de Quental. The mother country has been somewhat surpassed in this respect lately by Brazil. Frequenters of Lisbon bookshops are bound to notice the large number of foreign works, fictional and nonfictional, for sale in both the original language and in translations.

Scholarly life, though somewhat handicapped under the dictatorship, was by no means extinguished, for Salazar, after all, was a professor and a scholar. His regime saw the publication of the best encyclopedia ever published in the Portuguese language, a work completed after his death. The Portuguese Academy continues to produce scholarly works in science, history, and the arts. The Geographical Society of Lisbon, founded in 1875 to stimulate interest in the overseas possessions with a view to their extension in Africa, continues with its bimonthly *Boletim*, a learned review to which foreign scholars frequently contribute in their own languages.

Portugal does good work in the biological sciences, especially of the tropical kind, because of its continuing retention of considerable African possessions. It has not been outstanding in chemistry and physics, because these are expensive and require elaborate equipment costing more than Portuguese institutions or individuals can generally afford. In surgery, Dr. António Egas Moniz was awarded a Nobel Prize in 1949 for a brain operation he called prefrontal leucotomy.

Foreign and national students of Portuguese culture are highly indebted to the late Calouste Gulbenkian, the Armenian oil magnate who came to love Portugal and spent his final years there. He established the private Gulbenkian Foundation, which subsidizes Portuguese cultural studies, pays for visiting professorships, and awards fellowships to those who offer worthwhile projects for study. The Foundation program, at first only cultural, was later extended to include the social and economic development of Portugal. The direction of the Foundation is Portuguese, but some of the main beneficiaries have been students from the United States.

NATIONAL TRAITS AND RECREATIONS

The Portuguese may be the most courteous people in the world; they go far out of their way to help a stranger or to help each other. They apologize for every trivial incident they fear may give offense, and it is not uncommon to hear one laborer, dressed in working clothes, beg another's pardon for accidentally jostling while both stand uncomfortably on the rear platform of a crowded street car. "Disculpe" (excuse me) is one of the most frequently heard words of the Portuguese language. People of the serving class, unless they are old acquaintances, habitually use the formal mode of address, rather than the familiar, when speaking to each other. One matter that strikes the foreigner less favorably is the exploitation servants frequently undergo at the hands of employers. Women and girls from rural sections, whose lives have consisted of hard work and poverty, usually expect and experience the same in the towns and the homes of the more prosperous.

Cooking and cuisine are matters about which tastes differ, but those of Portugal would suit most palates. Breakfast usually consists of fruit or juice, rolls, and coffee; lunch and dinner resemble each other, though the midday meal is lighter. A typical Portuguese dinner consists of soup, fish and meat courses, and excellent bread, with a dessert of fruit and perhaps cheese. Law requires hotels serving meals and *pensões* (boarding houses) to include a reasonable amount of inexpensive wine, white or red, as the customer prefers. This goes with the repast; the diner may order something better at additional expense if he chooses. Portugal customarily dines late, though not so late as Spain. The Spanish dinner hour may be at 10 o'clock or even midnight; in Portugal it is around eight. The lateness in both countries cannot altogether apply to laboring people, who must start work at dawn or earlier.

Drunkenness is the least of Portugal's problems, for although it is a major wine-producing country, the people are noted for their sobriety. They consume wine steadily, but customarily only with meals, and what they drink is of low alcoholic content. It would be foolish to say that no one in Portugal overindulges, but in taverns and bars one seldom hears conversation become loud. Portuguese brandy is strong, but does not seem to command a great popular sale.

The Portuguese theater, which flourished in the sixteenth century and again in the nineteenth, is in a dormant period at present. Only rarely is a national stage play seen, and even presentations of translated foreign dramas are unusual. The influence of the legitimate theater is seen in motion-picture houses, where each program is divided into three parts with two intermissions, in the old manner of a three-act play. Because Portugal produces few films, the pictures are mostly Italian, French, English, and American. The language of the producing country is heard on the screen with running Portuguese translations, more or less in time with the actors' voices, appearing below. Newsreels are often Brazilian and so offer no language barrier. The picture public is well acquainted with the screen heroes and glamor girls of other countries.

Portugal is a music-loving country and it seems surprising that, except for folksongs, so little music is national. The National Theater of São Carlos in the center of Lisbon, with a capacity of 1,700 and dating from 1793, has almost yearly presented operas in which the world's greatest singers have appeared. Yet no Portuguese operatic composer has either enjoyed fame in his own land or commanded interest abroad. The recent *Concise Oxford Dictionary of Opera* mentions only a certain Leal Moreira, whose long-forgotten *Vingança da Gitana* (*Gypsy's Vengeance*) was performed at São Carlos the year after its opening. Italian opera is by far the favored kind in Portugal, and instrumental and symphonic music is invariably foreign.

A form of musical entertainment still popular in Portugal is the *fado*, a song of many verses that tells a story, frequently doleful. Because it requires only a guitar accompaniment and the tunes are simple, imposing no great tax on the voice, many can sing such ballads, but there are skilled professionals who perform in nightclubs, hotels, and for radio; television is still rare in Portugal. The tourist should realize, however, that most of the fados he hears are modernized and commercialized for his benefit.

Although the recent interest in soccer football has caused the old sport of bullfighting to decline in popularity, many are still faithful to it. The Portuguese bullfight differs from its Spanish and Mexican counterpart in that the *toiro* (bull) is neither killed nor seriously injured. The spectacle is one of expert horsemanship in which the rider teases the bull, whose horns are capped, and deftly eludes when the animal charges. He plants the darts, or *bandarilhas*, but these scarcely penetrate the skin. The *toiro* is apt, after a time, to grow weary of the whole affair, whereupon teenage boys rush on and stimulate him to further action. The boys run the only risks involved as they leap on the bull's back, pull his tail, and are in danger of being trampled. When one bull has lost all interest, he is taken from the arena and a fresh one and another horseman resume the entertainment.

RURAL LIFE

The previous descriptions have dealt principally with city and town life; something must now be said of the countryside. The picture there is not bright, nor does there seem much chance of improvement in the near future. The following dietary figure represents the Portuguese average: 2,670 calories of food a day, as opposed to 2,999 in France and 3,210 in Switzerland. The Portuguese average does not seem bad for sedentary occupations, but it is insufficient for those doing physical labor. Furthermore, it is an average for the entire nation; most farmers and farm laborers consume much less than that. It explains to an extent why work goes slowly and is often performed haphazardly. Add to this the fact that diet is ill-balanced and one explanation is provided of the prevalence of tuberculosis and the high death rate.

As long ago as 1887, Joaquim Pedro de Oliveira Martins, an engineer, historian, and economist who brought an emotional approach to all three subjects, said, when presenting a rural development program to the national legislature:

> At the moment when Portugal started on the road to discoveries, conquests, and colonization; from that very moment there began what we can call the Portuguese rural question. Until then the efforts of the governments were directed almost exclusively to economic development; from then on they gave preference to the overseas lands. And when the end came to the maritime epic, with the loss of the Orient and the separation of Brazil, we were obliged to look at our own country; the spectacle it offered us was desolating.
>
> In the north we have an agriculture that is little more than gardening (meaning very small scale), a very dense population, an abundance of emigration. . . . On the southern coast, in the south-central, and the entire length of the eastern frontier, we see steppes similar to those of Russia and deserts like the Sahara. . . . One can say that the oblique course of the Tagus separates inhabited Portugal from desert Portugal, cultivated Portugal from abandoned Portugal.

And the first necessity of our internal economy is to reestablish the equilibrium between these two halves, to unify them and transport what is lacking—men and capital—into the deficient regions.[1]

Though Martins said this a long time ago, the situation he denounced still holds true to some degree. No real effort was made to remedy it during the last stormy decades of the monarchy or from 1910 to 1926, the years of the first republic. The Salazar regime made very few attempts at reform, because it meant expensive geometric surveys of the land; the only surveys made depended largely on the memories and often inadequate knowledge of various people. The proprietors of *latifundios* (big estates) showed themselves hostile to all attempts to change the existing situation. The president of the Corporation of Agriculture is reported to have said, in substance, addressing technicians who had urged reform: "Very well, Senhores technicians, divide, dismember, refashion our family cultivations, but the day when someone tries to take possession of these new farms, well, so much the worse for him; the land is ours and we shall receive this thief, that usurper, with machine-gun bullets." [2] The threat seems to have been no empty one; it is said that under pretense of fighting Communism, which would certainly dispossess them, the proprietors have assembled arsenals and formed their own private armies.

A Salazar six-year plan to irrigate the Alentejo with water from the Guadiana River in order to raise living standards and get away from "dry" wheat farming was much talked about but came to little at the time the dictator was incapacitated. The evident reasons were the cost of the colonial war in Africa, the large sums spent on the Salazar Tagus bridge, and the fact that the project was expected to be financed largely by Germans, who proved lukewarm about it and preferred to invest in industry. The Germans wished also to have the management of the Alentejo project, which the Portuguese government refused to allow.

Portugal imports food, especially cereals, which would be unnecessary if the national agriculture were more scientifically and intelligently practiced. Part of the reason for shortages is the low physical condition of the poor farmer, who exists on an inadequate diet. Another is this farmer's discouragement with the miserable re-

1. Christian Rudel, *Le Portugal et Salazar*, pp. 27–28.
2. *Ibid.*, p. 29.

wards he gets for his labor. A few marketing cooperatives exist, but the ordinary middleman is a businessman who buys cheaply and sells at a great profit. One example is that of potatos, which the middleman buys at the rate of 30 *centavos* per kilogram and sells for two *escudos*, almost seven times as much. As a result, the annual yield of potatos has dropped until Portugal now imports them.

With life so unrewarding at home, the stronger Portuguese workers often emigrate abroad, and this loss of young laborers is felt keenly in the northern rural districts, some of which seem in danger of being populated mostly by the very young and the old. Much of the emigration is clandestine because of the known hostility of the government to such departures. Efforts to divert them to Angola and Mozambique, where they would remain under the Portuguese flag, have had little success, especially since the beginning of the native revolts that have made life more hazardous there. They go by the thousands to France, especially to the Paris vicinity, where, lacking education and skills, they can do only the humblest and most poorly paid work. Even this they seem to find preferable to the lives they would lead at home. Lately many have gone to Canada. If the departure of young men continues, it will eventually have an effect on the number available as soldiers.

From the government's point of view, the compensating factor in the situation has been that it drains off unemployed agricultural workers and probably lessens discontent in Portugal's labor circles. At home, the idle farm hands would drift into the main cities and furnish ready-to-hand recruits for agitators. Then too, if the emigrants come back they bring money, or, if they do not, they send it to their impoverished relatives.

CONCLUSION

In the early 1970s, Portugal seemed to have reached a crossroad, with its future course undetermined. The dictator who had governed for two generations had gone, and his successor, Caetano, appeared to promise significant changes, but how great they would be remained to be seen. Caetano had apparently gained control of the National Union, the party that had backed Salazar and supported him in office for so long. Despite some changes, superficial thus far, the government remained in essence a dictatorship, and there was no visible sign that Caetano's hold on the country was slipping or that any considerable segment of the population desired his removal. Meanwhile, the major problems of the country remained as before; poverty, ill health, need of industry at home, and an unstable situation in the overseas possessions.

2

Origins and Distant Past

THE FIRST INHABITANTS

Artifacts unearthed in Portugal show that the country went through both an Old and a New Stone Age, though the remains are few compared to those of Spain. In prehistoric times, just as in later eras, Portugal lay to one side, out of the major (Stone Age) culture currents, and was probably less populated than most of the rest of Europe.

A people whose main branch came later to be called Iberians moved into the Spanish peninsula between 2000 and 1000 B.C. They came either from North Africa or from Mediterranean Europe to the east and were slight and rather dark of complexion. Their basic organizational unit was the tribe, and they lived by hunting and fishing, gathering the fruits and nuts that nature provided, and practicing crude agriculture.

Bands of Celts, a taller, blonder people of Indo-European stock, entered Spain through the Pyrenees passes in about 900 B.C. as part of the great racial migration that saw them eventually settle in Gaul and the British Isles. Some Celts invaded Portugal, where less is known of them than of their life and history in Spain. They herded pigs, sheep, cattle, and goats, raised wheat, barley and flax, and mined various metals including iron. Western Celts, mixed with the Iberians in blood and culture, were known as *Lusitani,* and were a warlike agri-

18

cultural people, dwelling apart from the other Celtiberians, as the fused inhabitants of Spain came to be called. Their homeland, *Lusitania*, corresponded roughly to modern Portugal.[1]

Phoenician seaborne traders began visiting Spain in about 1000 B.C. They established Mediterranean coastal settlements, without penetrating far inland, and seem to have left the Lusitanian area alone. Greek traders came a few centuries later and founded their own Mediterranean towns for traffic with the interior inhabitants.

Carthage, a daughter city of Phoenician Tyre, ultimately affected Spain more than had the earlier traders. The Carthaginians, a major power and closer, for a time dominated much of the peninsula. They took over the older Phoenician settlements and in the interval between the First and Second Punic Wars (241–218 B.C.) brought southern and eastern Spain somewhat under control. Their influence barely touched Lusitania, which had no apparent part in the great war with Rome that Hannibal of Carthage precipitated in 218. He invaded Italy with an army largely composed of Spanish mercenaries that may have included Lusitanians, but when the Romans counterattacked the Carthaginians in Spain, they confined their operations to the Mediterranean coast.

THE ROMAN PERIOD

The war ended in 202 with Hannibal defeated, Carthage prostrate, and Rome in possession of eastern Spain. The republic then conquered the entire peninsula, slowly and region by region. Eventually the Romans reached Lusitania, which proved to be the hardest conquest of all. A war chief of the Lusitani named Viriathus, originally a simple shepherd, proved more than a match for the legions and defeated them in battle after battle. The Romans never vanquished this heroic leader and finally bribed disloyal followers of his to murder him as he slept in 139 B.C. Some Portuguese have considered Viriathus their first national leader for independence, but this is far-fetched because he thought only in tribal terms and campaigned as much outside Lusitania as within it.

Roman mastery of Spain, except for isolated spots, was complete

---

1. For a good survey of prehistoric Portugal, see Dan Stanislawski, *The Individuality of Portugal*, pp. 60–93. Paul MacKendrick's *The Iberian Stones Speak: Archaeology in Spain and Portugal* reveals what is known of Portuguese archaeology from the Stone Age to the late Roman period.

by 19 B.C., and meanwhile the republic had become an imperial
monarchy under Augustus, whose successors ruled it as part of their
great empire until the fifth Christian century. Portugal, with the rest
of the peninsula, became part of the Latin- and Greek-speaking culture that included the entire Mediterranean basin. Changes came
that proved enduring; the Romans brought their Latin speech, of
which Portuguese is in some respects the oldest vernacular branch.
They also brought their own pagan religion, though this had come
to be taken lightly by the Roman rulers, who required respect for
Jupiter only because he stood as a symbol of their government.

Christianity may, in a sense, be called a Roman contribution,
because without the empire, which made travel and communication
easier, missionary effort would have been much slower. Little is
known of the Lusitanian religious beliefs and the conquest probably
contributed to sweeping most of them away. There had been conversions to Christianity in Spain by the second century, but ground
was gained more slowly in Portugal. There is no mention of Christian
communities there before 300, but at about that time a Bishop of
Évora attended a church conference near Granada and his existence
implies that Christianity had had some years of growth. Emperor
Diocletian, before the end of his reign in 305, waged the final un-
successful persecution of Christians, to which Portugal contributed
martyrs. The next important emperor, Constantine, made Christianity a tolerated religion, and in 391 Theodosius made it the state
church and disestablished paganism without expressly forbidding it.

Rome built a number of its famous roads through Portugal, in-
troduced its own style of classical architecture, and improved peninsular agriculture. The olive and grape, probably brought by the
Phoenicians, were nevertheless scarce until the Romans increased
their cultivation. Wheat had been raised by the Celtiberians, especially in the Algarve, but the Romans stimulated greater production. Roman law entered with the conquerors, and though its influence waned during the invasions after Rome's fall, it was ultimately
the basis of the Portuguese legal code.

SWABIANS AND GOTHS

Soon after the year 400, the weakening of the Roman imperial
structure and withdrawal of legions from the Rhine frontier enabled
various Teutonic peoples to cross the river and invade Gaul. Among

those who crossed the Pyrenees and entered Spain were the Suevi, or Swabians, who concentrated their efforts in the northwest, which included the Portuguese Minho Valley, and made Braga (originally *Bracara Augusta*) their capital. Most important of the Germans were the Visigoths, who, from their original eastern home, invaded Italy, and in 410 sacked Rome itself. Induced by the remnant of the Roman government to transfer to Spain, they established a kingdom there in 414. Besides Spain, except for the Swabian district, this included much of Gaul, and the Visigothic ruler Euric (467–485) thus possessed the largest kingdom in western Europe. Soon after his death, most of the territory north of the Pyrenees was seized by the Franks, and the Visigothic realm was thereafter confined to Spain, which it possessed completely after conquering and absorbing the Swabians.

The new German rulers of the peninsula did not altogether sweep away Roman civilization, which they had learned to admire. Inevitable deterioration occurred under the semibarbaric Goths, but there was little wanton destruction or deliberate obliteration of culture. One barrier between the conquerors and the Hispano-Roman provincials for a time seemed insurmountable. The Goths had become Christian through missionary effort before entering the empire, but had accepted the Arian form, which differed in some respects from Roman Catholicism and was considered heretical by the Romans. The major difference was the Arians' refusal to grant Christ equal rank with God, which meant denial of the Catholic Trinity. The beliefs could not be reconciled, and there was bitterness between the adherents. The two nevertheless existed side by side until most of the Germans adopted the Roman form around the year 600.

The Gothic kingdom had its capital at Toledo at the center of the peninsula. The kings, whose predecessors had been little more than war chiefs, often lacked ability and displayed small understanding of their own royal interests. They parcelled out much of the land among their leading followers, which naturally reduced their revenues. The kings, except for a few able ones, were not very powerful and had limited control over their vassals. The monarchy, by tradition inherited from the old tribal times, was elective, and much of Visigothic political history was filled with contests for the throne, the last of which caused the kingdom to fall.

Intellectual life did not altogether cease in Spain during the three centuries of Gothic rule, although the principal contributors were the Romanized subject peoples. Orosius of Tarragona (fifth century), born in Portuguese Braga, was a noted theologian and scholar. He wrote a universal history, as he understood it, directed against the pagans who continued to exist in his time. During the seventh century, Gothic kings felt the need of a law code harmonizing the divergent legal notions of Goths and Romans. Accordingly, one was written in Latin with the purpose of abolishing laws on either side that prevented the amalgamation of the two peoples. This compilation, popularly called the "Laws of the Goths," was a great piece of legislation but did not bring the two sides much closer together. Styles of dress remained different, the Goths wearing trousers and the provincials wearing robes—differences that ultimately meant the distinction between warriors and priests. The Goths wore long hair and the Romans clipped theirs, and to have a haircut meant disqualification from the higher offices of state.

The kingdom was severely weakened by the end of the seventh century. The military vigor of the Goths had perhaps declined, and royal succession disputes lessened their unity and sapped their strength. By the opening of the next century Spain lay divided and ready for the next conquerors who, like the Carthaginians almost a millennium earlier, came from Africa.

The Arabs

The Prophet Mohammed preached his new religion, Islam, in Arabia, and by his death in 632 A.D. much of that peninsula had accepted his political and religious authority. His successors, the Caliphs, undertook a program of world conquest in the name of Allah and Islam, and by 700 their forces had swept across north Africa and subdued Morocco. They crossed to Spain in 711 and defeated Roderick, the last Visigothic king, largely because of the treachery of his own nobility. Within a few years, the Arabs, strengthened by many north-African Berber converts, swept through Spain and reached the Pyrenees.[2] Though repulsed in an invasion of Gaul, or France, in 732, they consolidated their power in Spain and presently seceded from the main Caliphate governed from Baghdad in Mesopotamia and later built a brilliant Muslim civilization.

2. The Arab conquest of Spain is expertly covered by E. Levi-Provençal, *España Musulmana hasta la Caida del Califato de Córdoba*, trans. from the French by Emilio García Gómez.

As to how Portugal fared in all this, the record is dim. It was conquered by the Muslims, although Arab authority was weaker in the north than in the south, where the Algarve (*Al-Gharb*) and the Alentejo, both hot, dry lands, were more to the invaders' liking. Lisbon and Oporto both became Muslim cities, but Arab rule scarcely extended beyond the Douro, north of which lay an almost unpopulated region. Lisbon was surrounded by a strong wall and had a castle citadel, but seems to have been less important than Oporto, which, in early Muslim times, guarded the northern frontiers. An undated document mentions capture of the city of Portucale by Alfonso I of Asturias about the middle of the eighth century, but this Christian occupation was brief and Oporto returned, for the time, to Muslim hands.[3]

Meanwhile a nucleus of Christian resistance had been set up in the Cantabrian mountains by a Gothic noble called Pelágio by the Portuguese and Pelayo by the Spaniards. His original band of followers was joined by other fugitives whom the Muslims at first ignored. But in 722, sensing danger, the Arabs sent a small column struggling up the mountain pass to the Caves of Covadonga. Pelágio ambushed and routed the Muslims and thus won the first Christian victory over the hated invaders. Though the military significance of the battle was small at the time, it lifted Christian morale and may truly have marked the first step in the reconquest of the peninsula.

Pelágio's successors became kings of Asturias and then of León, and acquired Galicia, north of Portugal. They raided and sometimes held the regions between the Minho and Douro Rivers, which included the towns of Braga, Oporto, and Guimarães. In the late tenth century, the Muslims, or Moors, as the Christians generally called them, waged a strong counteroffensive that nearly destroyed all the northern Christian states, which now included Navarre and Barcelona. Fortunately for the future of Spain and Portugal, the last great Islamic military leader died in 1002 without completing his task, and soon afterward the Spanish Muslims, no longer able to check the Christian advance, broke into petty independent states. Asturias and León presently united with the newer Castile to the east, and because Castile became the larger of the two, it will be convenient henceforth to speak of the kingdom of Castile and León.

3. The greater part of what is known of Oporto in the Arab period is furnished by Damião Peres et al., *História da Cidade do Porto*, I, 71–84.

In the course of the eleventh century, and especially under the powerful Alfonso VI (1065–1109), this combined kingdom expanded steadily southward. During Alfonso's reign, Portugal was born and began to take shape.

3

The Appearance of Portugal

There is a long-standing debate among historians over the reasons for independent Portugal's emergence in the twelfth century. It was originally a feudal dependency of León, and at first glance there is little to distinguish it from other such appendages—hence its emergence would seem to have been an historical accident. On the other hand, a case can be made for a Portuguese individuality, present and growing long before independence came. Although no real physical frontier exists on most of the Portuguese-Spanish border, the far north, where Portugal originated, does possess a dividing barrier in the Trás-os-Montes. Both beliefs have had their spokesmen. Alexandre Herculano, the nineteenth-century Portuguese historian, could find no explanation of his country's origin except accident. His opinion was generally accepted for years, but more recent Portuguese writers have emphasized differences in their ancestral culture extending at least back to early medieval times.

PORTUGUESE EMERGENCE

Alfonso VI of Castile and León possessed Galicia, just north of Portugal, a turbulent and out-of-the-way place. In order to have a reliable governor there, Alfonso bestowed this area on Raymond, son of a Burgundian count. The Portuguese area, south of the Minho, went to Raymond's relative, Henry, also from Burgundy, and with it the hand in marriage of Alfonso's illegitimate daughter, Teresa. Henry unquestionably owed his elevation to the older Raymond, but his own line was to have the important future. He proved to be both ambitious and a political opportunist. When Alfonso died in 1109, confusion reigned in León, and until his own death in about 1112, Henry backed whichever Leonese faction suited him at the moment, changed sides whenever convenient, and became virtually independent.

He left his widow, Teresa, and a three-year-old son, Afonso, surnamed Henriques after his father. The mother at first governed Portugal and emulated her deceased, but apparently unmourned husband by paying little attention to Leonese sovereignty. This may have pleased her subjects; what displeased them was her acceptance of a Galician lover, Fernando Peres, whom she may have secretly married. The Peres influence especially antagonized the Portuguese landed magnates, who gravitated to the support of young Afonso, now a precocious teenager determined not to be thrust aside by an unpopular Galician. The boy awaited a favorable moment and, with his backers, defeated Teresa and Peres in 1128 and exiled them from Portugal.

Afonso, with the title of count, first ruled his inheritance from Coimbra. He meant to enlarge his dominion, but for a few years seemed uncertain about the direction the expansion should take. Before seriously attacking the Muslims south of the Mondego River, he fought both León and its Galician tributary in hopes of gaining territory at their expense. Such actions rather spoil his reputation as a devoted crusader, even though the wars were partly forced upon him.

He won some sort of victory over the Muslims at Ourique, near Santarém, in 1139. Although the battle was small and lacking in notable results, it became exalted in Portuguese legend. Modern opinion is that Afonso won a victory in a border raid that did the enemy small damage. A medieval chronicler, writing long after the battle, magnified the Muslim host to enormous size and said that Henriques, with a handful of cavaliers, routed these enemies. More miraculous than the victory was the reported appearance of crucified Christ to Afonso to speak words of encouragement and incitement.[1]

1. The Battle of Ourique, historical and legendary, is covered by Tomaz da Fonseca, *D. Afonso Henriques e a Fundação da Nacionalidade Portuguesa*, pp. 165–70, 393–96.

Even before Ourique, Afonso had styled himself king of the Portuguese, which meant secession from León. Next, feeling the need of strong backing, he turned to the papacy and offered his new kingdom as a feudal fief of the Holy See. Pope Eugenius III accepted the homage but did not address him as royal for fear of offending Castile-León. Not until 1179, near the end of Afonso's long reign, did Pope Alexander III acknowledge his kingship.

THE CAPTURE OF LISBON

Times were favorable for Portuguese expansion southward. The Almoravid dynasty that had briefly reunited Moorish Spain had weakened, and a vigorous offensive by Afonso soon brought his frontier southward to the Tagus. He captured Santarém in 1147 and Lisbon later the same year. Lacking siege equipment, he could not have taken the latter strong-walled city by himself but fortunately had the help of an army of Englishmen, Germans, and Flemings bound for Palestine and the Second Crusade. They stopped at Oporto and were persuaded by Afonso to join him for the capture of Lisbon. After the city fell, most of the northerners went their own way, but some leaders chose to remain in Portugal, where Afonso liberally endowed them with feudal estates from the new lands he had gained.

The fall of Lisbon made nearby areas impossible to defend. Afonso swept well beyond the Tagus and took Alcácer, while Évora was captured for him by a free-lance fighter. The king pressed to the Algarve itself, but his fortunes declined in later years. He made the mistake of trying to capture Badajoz, where he received a wound and underwent temporary imprisonment. The Almohads, new African invaders who had replaced the Almoravids and had given fresh vigor to Moorish Spain, made a counteroffensive against Portugal, and when Afonso died in 1185 his southern boundary had considerably receded.

The successors of Afonso Henriques, within sixty-four years after his death, extended the frontiers of Portugal to its present limits. The immediate heir, Sancho I (1185–1211), was over thirty when his father died and for years, during the old king's senescence, had been the effective ruler. He did not aspire to be altogether a conqueror and showed more interest in populating his southern lands, which lay comparatively empty because of the raids and counter-raids of Christians and Moors. He accomplished enough of this to be remembered as *O Povoador* (The Colonizer). He presently undertook campaigns, however, and captured Silves in the Algarve, only to lose it when the Almohads reacted vigorously and regained most of the southern conquests of Afonso Henriques, limiting Portugal, except for Évora, to the Tagus frontier. But the Almohad power soon ended, for in 1212, just after Sancho's death, a coalition of Christian states, including Portugal, overwhelmingly defeated the Africans at Las Navas de Tolosa. Muslim Spain never produced another strong military state, and resistance to Portuguese expansion weakened until, in 1249, Sancho's grandson Afonso III (1248–1279) overran the Algarve and penetrated to the sea. This ended the Portuguese reconquest, and there could be no further expansion in Europe, where Castile, larger and stronger than Portugal, blocked the way.

O Rei Lavrador

The most successful reign in Portugal's medieval history, and the longest except for Afonso Henriques', was that of Denís (1279–1325). He became known as *O Rei Lavrador* (The Farmer King) because of his great interest in agriculture, which he considered the true source of national wealth. Denís undertook to show the nobles, who tended to despise all pursuits but war, the importance of cultivating their lands. He instilled the same lesson into the monastic and military orders, also the owners of large tracts, and insisted that uncultivated areas be placed in the hands of families of small farmers who would make them produce. Denís caused marshes to be drained and trees planted to furnish lumber for construction and shipbuilding. Thanks to his efforts, Portugal eventually was able to raise grains for export, and these, with olive oil, wine, salt, salted fish, and dried fruit, were traded to Flanders, England, Brittany, and Catalonia. In return, Portugal received iron, copper, tin, lead, brass, linen cloth, and silk. This trade, often carried in Portuguese ships, and the quality of his coinage, caused Denís to be considered a rich king, although contemporaries certainly exaggerated his wealth.

He had abundant other interests, including the spread of education and the encouragement of literature. Following the example of his maternal grandfather, Alfonso the Learned of Castile, he ordered legal documents and judicial acts' written henceforth in the language of the people instead of Latin, thus stimulating the use of Portuguese as a literary vehicle. Denís founded a university at Lisbon in 1290 and moved it to Coimbra eighteen years later, after which it had another sojourn at Lisbon before its final transfer to Coimbra in 1527. Students of all ages attended, because the desire to learn sometimes proved stronger in mature men than in youths,[2] and the charter gave faculty and students unusual privileges.

The life of Denís, if prosperous, was not always serene. His queen, Isabel of Aragon, of undeniable virtue, was later canonized but had a way of interfering in politics that the king found irksome. Denís had trouble with the secular clergy over the amount of land the Church had accumulated, some of which he ordered sold to private individuals. As he grew elderly, he had to cope with quarrels among his legitimate and illegitimate sons, who sometimes rebelled when he sided with one or another.

The Last Burgundians

The House of Burgundy ruled Portugal until 1383; ably for two generations following Denís, but incompetently thereafter. Afonso IV (1325–1357) was more of a fighting monarch than his father had been, but also gave much attention to the commercial interests of Portugal. He kept on good terms with the Italian cities of Genoa and Venice, whose trading fleets now made regular voyages to the Low Countries, northern France, and England. Lisbon and other Portuguese harbors lay conveniently on their route, offering shelters for reprovisioning and watering. Afonso is known to have granted trade privileges to the Florentine banking house of Bardi, as well as to the Lombards of Milan and Piacenza, which evidently included safeconducts for individuals and the merchants collectively. Near the end of his reign, Afonso gave general commercial privileges to the Genoese, Milanese, and Piacentines, and these were confirmed by his successor, Pedro I.[3]

Portugal now had a merchant fleet of its own for northern trade, and as early as Denís' time was beginning to acquire a navy. The noted Genoese seaman, Emmanuele Pessagno, made a contract with the king in 1317, by which he undertook to bring twenty captains from his city to command royal ships. Under the Portuguese form

2. A. H. de Oliveira Marques, *Daily Life in Portugal in the Late Middle Ages*, p. 232.
3. Charles Verlinden, *The Beginnings of Modern Colonization. Eleven Essays with an Introduction*, pp. 99–100.

of his name, Peçanha, he conducted a fleet that visited the known Canaries and the perhaps unknown Madeiras and Azores. Although no annexation or colonization followed, the Peçanha voyage may be called the first step toward overseas expansion.

New invaders from Morocco, called Benimerines or Marinids, had entered Spain to make conquests and bolster their co-religionists, who were on the retreat before the Christians. Alive to the danger, Afonso allied with Castile and led 1,000 mounted lancers to help defeat the Africans. At the Battle of the Salado River in 1340, the Christians routed the Benimerines. There is some evidence that the Salado was the first European battle that saw cannon used, presumably by the Castilians. If so, the guns did not decide the day, which was won by conventional medieval shock tactics.

The close of Afonso's reign involved him in the saddest romantic episode of Portuguese history, that of his son and heir, Prince Pedro, and a Galician lady-in-waiting, Inés de Castro. Pedro's second wife had died giving birth to Fernando, later king of Portugal, and the prince then bestowed his affections on the young Castro lady, who bore him two sons and a daughter. Inés is described as being extraordinarily beautiful and gentle; she loved Pedro but did not aspire to be his wife or to elevate her bastard children above the legitimate Fernando. Yet her brothers were ambitious men desirous of making the most of the heir apparent's passion for their sister. The situation worried the elderly Afonso, who vainly urged his son to marry again and remove the dangerous Castro influence. The king's counselors took every opportunity to stress the threat to the legitimate succession while Inés remained alive. The perturbed king finally resolved to kill her himself and went with armed followers to Coimbra, where Pedro had installed his mistress and their children in a luxurious house. Face to face with Afonso, Inés pleaded so eloquently for her life and the safety of the children, his grandchildren, that the king, who was not a cruel man, spared her and left. A short distance away the counselors renewed their arguments, and Afonso, changing his mind again, told them to do as they wished. They returned to the house and stabbed Inés to death. This much of the story seems reliable; legends and poetic accretions have obscured much of the rest.[4] Even if Inés was wholly innocent, the Castros were a dangerous brood, and if

4. The greatest poet of all, Camões, gives much real and imaginary detail regarding the episode in Os Lusiadas, canto 3.

Pedro was the romantic lover he seemed, he nevertheless had another mistress, Teresa Lourenço, on whom he sired a bastard during the lifetime of Inés.

Pedro, learning of the murder, rebelled against his father and found supporters, including the Castro brothers. Pedro's mother and a well-meaning prior acted as peacemakers and the prince finally returned to obedience with the feeling that he could await the time of vengeance on those responsible for Inés' murder. Two years later, Afonso's death made him king of Portugal.

Pedro I (1357–1367) began reigning with the determination to make the three slayers of Inés pay for their crime. They fled for their lives to Castile, but the new king arranged an extradition treaty with his neighbor and two were handed over to him; the third managed to disappear. Pedro put his two victims to a horrible death; then, as if realizing that the people were shocked at his barbarity, he declared that he and Inés had been secretly married and that their children were legitimate. The public remained unconvinced, and the day later came when one of these offspring was rejected for the throne because of his presumed bastardy.

For all his cruelty, Pedro left some favorable impression of his monarchical capacity. He earned the soubriquet *Justiceiro*, meaning rigorous or impartial, and had a constant interest in the courts and law enforcement. He was a gloomy man and his judgments, though severe, were not without meaning and a certain crude justice. Several of the cruel punishments he inflicted are remembered; in one case two of his friends robbed and murdered a Jew, and to make them confess Pedro threatened to lash them with whips. When they pleaded guilty and those around him begged that he spare their lives, Pedro muttered that: "from Jews they would proceed to Christians," and ordered them beheaded. Other punishments involved a bishop whom he mercilessly whipped for seducing a married woman and a rural squire he ordered to execution for wrecking the wine vat of a simple farmer.

These cases are mentioned to show both Pedro's sense of justice and his ferocious way of enforcing it. He has been called a madman, but other acts of his show considerable ability. He looked after the commercial interests of his kingdom and, by a treaty with France, obtained privileges for Portuguese merchants there. He protected foreign traders in his country, especially those of Catalonia, England, and Italy, and the nation increased in prosperity in the ten years he governed. There is little doubt that he suffered from epilepsy, which seldom causes death but may have been a contributory cause to his demise at the age of forty-seven.

Fernando (1367–1383), Pedro's only son by a legal wife, came to the throne when he was barely twenty-two. He proved a dismal failure as a ruler and with him the House of Burgundy ended. He first antagonized the king of Castile, Henry of Trastamara, by jilting his daughter, to whom he was affianced, in favor of beautiful Leonor Teles, niece of the Portuguese count of Barcelos. This brought disapproval by the Portuguese public because it threatened to cause war with Castile. The Teles lady had a husband, whom the young king drove into exile and whose marriage to Leonor he proclaimed void because the parties were related. The citizens, with reason, considered Leonor a woman of bad character, notwithstanding which the enamored ruler took her north, where adverse feeling seemed less strong, and there went through a marriage ceremony. The new queen at once began to confirm all fears by arranging for the torture and death of various detractors.

England now made its first prominent appearance in Portuguese affairs. John of Gaunt, Duke of Lancaster and son of Edward III, felt that he had a claim to the Castilian throne through his Spanish wife, and Fernando decided to ally with him.[5] Portugal became the principal sufferer in the new war; the English lent no direct support and the Castilian army captured Viseu and Coimbra, bypassed Santarém, and besieged Lisbon with the cooperation of a fleet that had entered the Tagus. The Lisbon citadel held out, but the best part of the city perished in a fire set by the invaders. Portugal seemed on the verge of extinction when Pope Gregory XI (1370–1378), the last to reign at Avignon, persuaded the two kings to make peace. Henry dictated the terms by which Fernando abandoned the English alliance, agreed to treat the English as enemies, promised to keep their ships out of his ports, and expel Castilian enemies of King Henry who had taken refuge with him. As a guarantee of good faith, he gave up certain territories and fortresses, as well as hostages, including Leonor's brother. Portugal for the moment had become a dependency of Castile.

Fernando had no thought of abiding by these humiliating terms. Once free of the invaders, he strengthened his armed forces, rebuilt

5. This English connection is covered in detail by P. E. Russell, *The English Intervention in Spain and Portugal in the Time of Edward III and Richard II.*

the walls of Lisbon and Oporto, and repaired damaged castles. Portuguese agriculture, so flourishing under Denís, had declined during the late disastrous war. The Law of the *Sesmarias* (uncultivated lands) now provided that in the future all suitable areas should be tilled and ordered confiscated those whose owners neglected to carry out the law. Fernando promoted commerce and Lisbon soon again became a thriving center for merchants. The English were not kept out long, for Henry of Castile died in 1377 and the one-sided treaty became a dead letter.

Shortly before he died, Fernando had considerably improved his political and economic situation, but seemingly could not consistently follow a constructive policy. He fought Castile again and gained nothing; another English alliance brought only misfortune. Leonor Teles, elevated to the Portuguese throne by the infatuation of Fernando, was unfaithful, and he fully knew of her carryings-on with João Fernandes Andeiro, Count of Ourém.

Fernando, still young in years, was prematurely aged and sick by 1383, and profoundly discouraged. By Leonor he had only a daughter, Beatriz. One of his final acts, the worst of many mistakes, was to betroth and marry the 11-year-old girl to John I of Castile, with whom he had recently fought. Until Beatriz could govern in person, subject to the will of her Spanish husband, Leonor, more unpopular now than ever, was to be regent following her husband's death. Then, as a recent American historian puts it: "Having steered the ship of state straight for the rocks and tied the helm fast, Fernando set sail in October 1383 on what we shall hope was his heaven-bound galley." [6]

6. Bailey W. Diffie, *Prelude to Empire: Portugal Overseas Before Henry the Navigator*, p. 72.

4 [1]

Medieval Portugal

THE GOVERNMENT

The medieval rulers of Portugal, as examples already given have shown, had power of life and death over their subjects and considered such power necessary because they exemplified the state. As in England, some distinction was made between "King" and "Crown," the first meaning the ruler as a private individual and the second the royal powers he wielded. It goes without saying that no ruler could altogether differentiate in practice. Portuguese jurists taught that the monarch recognized no human being superior and that in him resided the fountainhead of law. He customarily began his decrees with the words: "from our true knowledge and absolute power," and this high-sounding formula might be the preface to some very arbitrary ruling. Nevertheless, there was an institutional concept of royalty in which the monarch was thought of as representing the general interests.

The royal title was "King of the Portugals, King of the Portuguese, King of Portugal and of the Algarve." The rulers prided themselves on complete independence from the kings of Castile-León, and although Afonso Henriques had once paid homage to the papacy, this soon lost all meaning. The Holy Roman Empire pretended to some

1. This chapter is partly based on *História de Portugal: Edição Monumental* (hereinafter cited as *Edição Monumental* to avoid confusion with other works called *História de Portugal*), vol. II.

authority over the secular rulers of Europe, but in Portugal, as was generally true elsewhere, no attention was paid to this. The Portuguese kings did refrain for centuries from styling themselves "majesties," which emperors alone had the right to do, and were addressed by their subjects as *"altezas"* (highnesses). Unless unusual circumstances made it impossible, primogeniture governed succession to the throne, meaning that when a king died he was succeeded by his oldest legitimate son. There was no law forbidding female rulership as in France, but no woman reigned until the eighteenth century.

To help with the detailed tasks and drudgery of government, the monarchs at first had a small body of officials called the *curia regis*, which at times became a larger gathering of representatives of the principal classes. Early in the reign of Portugal's third king, Afonso II, one of these general assemblies received the popular name *côrtes*, after that of a similar slightly older body in Castile-León. Within a few decades a Portuguese côrtes came to consist of spokesmen from the clergy, the nobles, called *ricos-homens* (rich men), and the towns. The clerical representatives were the bishops, those of the nobility were the more important ricos-homens,[2] and the town members generally consisted of two from each community chosen by a form of election no longer known but probably varying from place to place. A côrtes somewhat resembled a parliament and, as was true of its English equivalent in the beginning, had no lawmaking powers; only the right to advise the king. However, it rapidly developed the habit of petitioning the sovereign for the redress of grievances, though the ruler was entitled to reject the requests. One of the principal concerns of the earlier côrtes members was money, of which the king often needed a greater supply than the ordinary sources of revenue provided. Because most of the national wealth was owned by those represented in the côrtes, its members often made their voices heard very effectively. Peasant farmers and laborers had no representation, unless the landed proprietors and the wealthy townsmen could be said to speak for them, which it is certain they generally did not.

Local government was rather a mixture of customs and principles. The original northern part of Portugal, where the customs of León were to some extent perpetuated, differed considerably from the south, which had been taken from the Moors. The Leonese institutions were for the most part old Visigothic ones; in the south these

2. This title later dropped out of use.

had disappeared during centuries of Moorish rule. A long-established nobility existed in the north; in the conquered southern parts the kings improvised as they went along. They conceded much of the land to followers on feudal terms but did much governing through royal councils. Where the nobles owned land, they tried to maintain their own courts and administer justice; the kings tried to encroach on this jurisdiction and substitute royal courts and judges.

Most of the Portuguese towns had existed in Roman times, but their medieval institutions were not inherited from Rome. The origins of city privileges (*forais*) are found in concessions granted by kings, nobles, and monastic orders. These often had to do with local administration of justice. Towns could have a single judge, sometimes more, to decide the major cases, besides *alcaides*, from the Arab *cadi*, for the lesser ones. The judges had powers for their own localities that went beyond ordinary judicial matters; they possessed a great deal of financial authority and within limits could act as lawmakers.

Despite the small size of Portugal, much of the land was only sparsely inhabited. Because of the recent uncertainty of life due to border wars, the people tended to live in cities or fortified places separated from each other by substantial distances. Sancho I and later rulers undertook to colonize these empty stretches, but progress came slowly. Medieval population figures are always unreliable, but Portuguese numbers are thought to have reached about 1 million in the fourteenth century.

The Church

The Portuguese Church as a distinct national institution independent of the Spanish branch begins with the See of Braga. This is the oldest diocese of the country and its archbishop has the title of Primate. Braga once had close ties with the See of Compostela in Galicia, but the two went in separate directions before Afonso Henriques seceded from León. Diego Gelmirez, Bishop of Santiago de Compostela, had tried to make himself primate of the entire Spanish peninsula on the grounds that St. James the Greater, brother of Christ, was buried there. The See of Braga resisted this claim and was backed by the Diocese of Oporto. Because the controversy occurred near the time of Afonso Henriques' political break with León, the religious split encouraged the growth of national feeling.

As Afonso and his successors carried their arms southward, the

Church took an important part in the conquest, and the military crusading orders, the Knights Templar and Knights Hospitaler, were often spearheads of the Portuguese advance. When Philip IV of France (1285–1314) persecuted the Templars and seized their property, and when Pope Clement V suppressed the order altogether in 1311, King Denís felt that Portugal still had uses for it. The papacy granted him the right to the lands and rentals of the Templars, and he proceeded to create a Portuguese substitute, the Military Order of Christ. Similar orders that came into existence about then were São Tiago, separate from the Spanish knights of the same name, St. John of the Hospital, loosely called Crato, and Avís. These knightly and monkish organizations, with men constantly under arms, long furnished almost the only standing army that Portugal possessed.

The Bishop of Braga for a time hoped to become the first ecclesiastical authority in the country, but the wish failed to materialize, for Coimbra was the national capital until it was superseded by Lisbon in 1422, and a convent there held the tombs of the earliest Portuguese kings. Possession of the university after 1308 gave Coimbra another important advantage over Braga. The conquests of Santarém and Lisbon in 1147 moved the Church's center of gravity southward, although Lisbon did not become the full-fledged center of Portuguese religion until centuries later.

Afonso Henriques consented to be a papal vassal and to pay, more for political than religious reasons, a tribute of four ounces of gold a year. His successors generally strove to keep on good terms with Rome. During the Great Schism (1378–1415), when there were rival Popes at Rome and Avignon, and briefly a third, Portugal steadily adhered to the claimant at Rome. The political balance of power accounted for this; as Castile followed France in recognizing the Avignonese pontiff, Portugal followed England, with which it was on better terms, in acknowledging Rome.

At the everyday level, the Church affected men's lives profoundly. Attendance at mass was general and frequent; noblemen were expected to hear mass daily, although this custom appears to have been abandoned by the fourteenth century. Evidently confession and taking the communion sacrament were infrequently practiced by the commoners. Portuguese religious texts stated that penitents, at a minimum, should confess between Epiphany Sunday and the beginning of Lent and commune on Easter Sunday. Examples of penances that have survived from medieval Portugal are severe; fifteen years of penitence for sodomy or copulation with animals; seven years for violation of any of the ten commandments.[3] Little is known of medieval sermons except that they were usually short and simple in tone.

THE ECONOMY

The southward conquests of the first Burgundian kings of Portugal failed to improve the living conditions of the conquered people. The Muslims had not forced the conversion of Christians in their territories, and many, over the centuries, had learned to dwell in contentment. Too often these Christians found that the conquering Portuguese made small distinction between the Moors and themselves and regarded both as legitimate prey. The northern newcomers seized all lands, and Christian inhabitants often found themselves reduced to servitude along with their Muslim neighbors. Understandably, many fought fiercely for the Islamites against the intruders.

It was fairly standard procedure for a region to be conquered by a king and then assigned to one of his companions-in-arms, either in outright ownership or the enjoyment of its revenue. With the land went ownership of all houses, cattle, agricultural tools, and human beings. Muslims often became slaves outright; Christians more likely became serfs bound to the land, their only protection being that they could not be expelled from it. Besides being tillers of the earth, serfs were used for household work in the castles or monasteries, or were made herdsmen or practitioners of such crafts as weaving, smithery, masonry, or baking. The increase of skilled labor among serfs had considerable bearing on the end of Portuguese serfdom, which was already declining by the thirteenth century.

The landscape was dotted with fortified buildings to give protection from raids by Moors or the all-too-frequent Christian marauders. A walled area surrounded the central structure, and when the alarm sounded, serfs and freemen took refuge within it. In peaceful times, the enclosure served as a community center in which orders were issued, disputes settled, and punishments inflicted.

The principal crops cultivated were grains and vines, besides many vegetables and fruits, including olives and chestnuts, which also grew wild. Agricultural products that had flourished in Muslim

3. A. H. de Oliveira Marques, *Daily Life in Portugal in the Late Middle Ages,* pp. 208–9.

Portugal often had Latin-derivative names, showing that they had been grown in Roman times.

Medieval Portuguese clothing was usually of linen from home-grown flax, or of wool from the coats of the numerous sheep. The custom of later poor Portuguese of working barefoot was evidently not practiced in the middle ages. Illustrations from those times showing agricultural scenes display all the laborers shod,[4] and a table of compulsory wages issued by Afonso III in 1253 made these include two pairs of shoes a year for every worker.

Cities and towns during the early centuries maintained themselves primarily by the agriculture of the surrounding areas, and many of the inhabitants still practiced farming in the vicinity. Tillers were at constant odds with raisers of livestock, who allowed their animals to wander destructively through the fields and orchards. Even city streets were not immune from inroads by the beasts, and municipal councils constantly passed ordinances to keep them out.

Much city marketing was done at *feiras* (fairs or markets), a word that came to mean in Portuguese the five weekdays, exclusive of Saturday and Sunday. These market-fairs were generally seasonal, depending on local conditions; they varied by communities and came in the slack times between the harvesting of crops. During the period between feiras, merchants travelled with their goods from place to place to satisfy local needs.

Medieval Portugal had its own coinage, though money was scarce. Coins minted in Constantinople, Moorish Spain, France, and León circulated and sometimes were melted down and reissued by Portuguese kings. The country produced little domestic gold, so the presumption is that most of the early coinage was of this reworked kind. Foreign trade was minimal in the early centuries, and the bulk of the gold must have been taken in war. Gold ceased to be coined in the thirteenth century and good silver coinage did not begin until the fourteenth. A substitute was *bilhão*, mostly copper with a thin silver alloy.[5]

Portuguese kings frequently debased the coinage by replacing money in circulation with coins made of metal of a less precious content. Announcement of a new issue would be accompanied by a law of price ceiling, which had little effect upon sellers. Prices rose so

4. Marques reproduces several illustrations of medieval peasants at work.
5. *Ibid.*, p. 9.

fast and such complaints poured in that rulers were sometimes obliged to abandon their debasement plans.

Moors and Jews, the non-Christian classes of the country, had great economic importance, and special laws existed to regulate their activities. They dwelt in restricted areas or quarters, with judges of their own to administer justice. Jews had control of most banking and moneychanging and, while forbidden to practice usury, managed to collect some interest. Muslims had been skilled agriculturists under their own regime and continued to be so under Christian rule.

5

The House of Avís

ALJUBARROTA

Fernando, before dying, named Leonor Teles regent for their daughter, Beatriz, and married the child to John I of Castile. Everyone knew that the marriage might mean the end of independent Portugal, and the weak Fernando had superstitious feelings of helplessness at the time. By her husband's will, Leonor could rule three years, until Beatriz reached the age of 14. She did not govern badly at first and seemed more popular than she had been in Fernando's lifetime. John of Castile had no intention of waiting, however, and meant to take the Portuguese crown at once. By his request, Leonor sent letters throughout Portugal ordering that Beatriz and John be acclaimed rulers. Her lover, João Fernandes Andeiro, was considered responsible for this, and a group of patriotic Portuguese resolved to remove him in the national interest. They selected as their leader John, Master of the Military Order of Avís, son of the late Pedro by Teresa Lourenço. Cooperating, with even greater determination than the Master, was aristocratic young Nuno Álvares Pereira, assisted by a number of patriotic commoners. The assassins (or liberators, as the case may be) entered the royal palace and stabbed Andeiro to death almost before the queen's eyes. The Lisbon public seemed to approve the act, and as John of Avís was now the leading candidate for the throne, some even proposed that he marry Leonor Teles. She wished

41

none of him, but the Master was informally proclaimed Defender and Governor of the Realm, after which he named several followers to administrative posts, the office of constable going to Nuno Álvares and that of chancellor to the noted jurist João das Regras. Meanwhile Portuguese opinion divided over the issue, the greater nobles generally favoring Leonor and John of Castile, the bishops being divided, and the commoners mostly accepting John of Avís.

The Castilian ruler invaded Portugal; Leonor gave him full support; and the Master and constable took charge of the defense. João das Regras appeared before a côrtes at Coimbra and convinced its members to accept John of Avís, henceforth John I, as their rightful king. Although his arguments had some weaknesses, most of the hearers were of the same frame of mind.

The issue was settled on the battlefield of Aljubarrota in August 1385. Nuno Álvares effectively commanded the Portuguese, and the new king fought bravely. Badly outnumbered and lacking in cavalry because so many aristocrats hung back, Álvares had at least the support of some 700 longbowmen recruited in England. Employing primarily defensive tactics, he won a decisive victory and put John of Castile to flight.[1] The war dragged on desultorily until 1411, but Aljubarrota had assured the Portuguese future.

John I

The new king was twenty-eight when the great victory placed him in secure possession of the throne, and now, as founder of a new dynasty, he needed a wife. Circumstances suggested an English princess, and the logical choice was Philippa of Lancaster, daughter of John of Gaunt and granddaughter of the late Edward III. The Treaty of Windsor-Westminster in 1386 established the historic Anglo-Portuguese Alliance, with an English guarantee of Portugal's independence. The following year, Duke John brought Philippa and an army to Portugal to renew his fight for the Castilian crown. The royal marriage took place, although John of Gaunt received little military help from his son-in-law and soon gave up his Spanish ambitions and went home.

John of Portugal and Philippa lived contentedly together until

1. For information about the Battle of Aljubarrota and the events surrounding it, see P. E. Russell, *The English Intervention in Spain and Portugal in the Time of Edward III and Richard II*, pp. 381–98.

her death in 1415, and meanwhile produced several able sons, the most important being Duarte (Portuguese for English Edward), heir to the throne; Pedro, later regent of the realm,[2] and Henrique, the famous Henry the Navigator.[3] The reign of John I witnessed an increase of royal power. A convincing proof is furnished by the king's infrequent summoning of the côrtes in later years, although he owed his throne originally to its loyalty at Coimbra: during one stretch of nine years he called no côrtes at all.

For thirty years after Aljubarrota, John's reign was generally peaceful. With the English departure, the Castilian war became spasmodic, and the king proved easygoing and anxious to avoid foreign trouble. Not until he neared age sixty did he take the field again, for reasons regarding which the Portuguese chroniclers are not unanimous.

Certainly the three grown princes, Duarte, Pedro, and Henry, urged the capture of Ceuta in Morocco, because they wished to win knightly spurs in genuine combat instead of the mock war of a tournament. Queen Philippa encouraged them and gave a crusading sword to each as she lay dying of plague when they departed. John was moved by these arguments, but he had other reasons, some private and some dictated by political and economic considerations. He had enjoyed fighting when young, and still had sufficient health and vigor for a last campaign. He possessed the means, for Portugal was now a maritime nation with a merchant navy trading to the northern countries and the Mediterranean. The upper classes, now reconciled to his rule, would welcome the spoils of conquest and gladly follow him to Africa. The burgesses, numerically predominant in the royal council, could see economic advantages for themselves in conquests overseas. Aggression in Spain would accomplish nothing; experience had shown that no gains there could be permanent. Africa seemed much more promising; Ceuta was the seaport commanding a large interior trade and in Portuguese hands might enrich John's kingdom. Its capture should not be postponed, because Castile had designs on Morocco and had commenced the occupation of the Canary Islands. Evidence strongly suggests that the main architect of the Ceuta plan was João Afonso, bourgeois minister of finance.[4]

2. Highly recommended reading about this prince is Francis M. Rogers' *The Travels of the Infante Dom Pedro of Portugal.*

3. A recent careful study of the work of Henry is found in Vitorino Magalhães Godinho's *A Economia dos Descobrimentos Henriquinos.*

4. *Ibid.*, p. 110.

Having decided, John concealed his destination until he was ready to strike. Military preparations in Portugal required three years, and Ceuta grew visibly uneasy. Yet the city lay unprepared when John landed his troops and made the assault in August 1415, and it capitulated after a brief resistance.

To John and his elder statesmen, the conquest of Ceuta was probably sufficient, but to the younger generation, headed by the princes, it was only a beginning. Because of them, the Moroccan enterprise is seen today as the prelude to Portugal's overseas expansion, which made it the first modern imperial power and made Lisbon briefly the commercial capital of Europe.

Reasons in addition to the ambitions of kings and princes impelled Portugal to undertake discoveries. The country lies at the southwest corner of Europe, facing the Atlantic with its back to Spain. It is a narrow coastal strip with a limited hinterland, beyond which no growth could be expected. Although it was perhaps not yet the maritime equal of several Mediterranean states, it had some seafaring tradition, and Lisbon had become a shipbuilding center. Like Spain, it had a crusading history and a desire to continue the offensive that had started at Ceuta. The urge to extend Christendom was strong in all Portuguese leaders from Prince Henry onward, varying with individuals but always present. The Prester John legend, dating from 1165, of a mighty Christian ally beyond Islam influenced Prince Henry, who identified the Prester with the ruler of Christian Abyssinia.

A powerful stimulus was the quest for wealth, which in Henry's time meant a search up African rivers for gold to remedy a currency shortage in Portugal. It meant the ambition of Portuguese sugar growers to expand their activity in favorable climates, the search for slaves both to man the sugar plantations and as an investment, and the enlargement of Portuguese sealing and fishing areas.[5]

Henry had carried sponsorship of discovery voyages well forward by his father's death in 1433. He was no navigator himself, but he sent out voyagers for discovery, and possessed financial resources, being Grand Master of the Order of Christ, which gave him not only a treasury but manpower for the galley ships he dispatched from Sagres or Lagos in southern Portugal. Besides means, he had leisure, for as a third son he was unlikely to be called to the throne.

5. *Ibid.*, pp. 80–81.

When Duarte became king, Henry's efforts had accomplished the rediscovery and colonization of the Madeiras, the discovery of the eastern Azores, and the tracing of the African coast to Cape Bojador in the present Spanish Sahara.

DUARTE AND AFONSO V

Duarte (1433–1438), the heir of John I, was middle-aged and already in failing health when he became king. During his brief reign, he depended heavily on the advice of his brothers Pedro and Henry, though he was talented and usually spoke the deciding word on questions of policy and action. Duarte approved of Henry's discovery work, but had no enthusiasm for more conquests in Morocco, which Henry and a younger brother, Fernando, constantly advocated.

The king's most important piece of legislation is called the "Mental Law" because of the assumption that it existed in the mind of John I before his death but was not promulgated in writing. Under Duarte it was written and called for the taking back by the crown of property which his father's over-generosity had distributed to supporters as a reward for allegiance during the Castilian invasion. The law emphasized the fact that the grants had not been made in perpetuity but reverted to the crown in default of male heirs. Duarte died too soon to enforce the law himself to any degree.

Always indulgent with his brothers, Duarte for once failed to speak the deciding word when, against his better judgment, he permitted Henry and Fernando to lead an expedition against Tangier in 1437. They had reasons for the undertaking, for in Muslim hands the city posed a standing threat to Portuguese possession of Ceuta. But Henry, who as the senior brother held command, mismanaged the operation, which he undertook with inadequate forces. Instead of besieging Tangier, he found himself besieged when large Moorish reinforcements gathered in his rear. To save what remained of the expedition, he begged a truce and left Fernando in enemy hands as a guarantee that Ceuta would be handed back. Henry returned humiliated to Portugal; Ceuta was not relinquished; and Fernando remained captive until his death eleven years later. Soon after Henry's return, Duarte died, reportedly of grief over the loss of Fernando.

Afonso V (1438–1481) was only six when his father's death made him king. The situation required a regent and the logical person was Pedro, though the boy-king's mother, Leonor of Aragon, hated the prince. The cause of her dislike is not altogether known, although Pedro was unquestionably a domineering individual suspected by some, probably mistakenly, of intending to usurp the throne. Leonor could not prevent his selection as regent by a côrtes at Lisbon, and after a time went to complaining in Castile, where she spent her last few years trying unsuccessfully to bring about a Spanish intervention in Portugal.

Pedro governed the kingdom successfully until Afonso reached the age of fourteen in 1446. As regent he cooperated with Henry in the discovery enterprises, which progressed rapidly. During the 1440s, Portuguese seamen pressed down the African coast to the mouths of the Senegal and Gambia Rivers, and soon after Pedro's death occurred the discovery of the Cape Verde Islands and coastwise progress to Sierra Leone.

Pedro came to a sad end. Leonor of Aragon had died in Spain, but other enemies existed in Portugal. Leading these was Afonso, Duke of Bragança, an illegitimate son of John I, born before his marriage to Philippa. Bragança resented the inferiority to his half brothers this bastardy caused, and above all resented Pedro, the head of the family. Young Afonso had already learned from his mother a hatred of the regent, even though he had married Pedro's daughter, and Bragança worked by slander and insinuation to bring about an open clash. When Pedro resigned the regency, he was not disposed to surrender all power to a teenaged boy and continued to behave in a lordly, independent manner. Bragança and his friends fanned the flames of hatred until matters came to civil war. Prince Henry tried too late to reconcile the parties; a battle took place at Alfarrobeira in May 1449 and the former regent was killed by a stray arrow from a crossbowman.

Fully on his own now, young Afonso gave Portugal a reign that was improvident and nearly disastrous. The elderly Henry perhaps exerted some restraining hand on his nephew until his own death in 1460, but the Prince Navigator was far from the equal of Pedro as an administrator and, like the young king, was given to romantic enterprises. They went together on an expedition against Alcazarseguer in Morocco and easily took the place, but it proved to be merely an expensive outpost to maintain. Later in the reign, Afonso captured Tangier and Arsila in Morocco, neglecting the great work of geographical discovery southward in Africa that Henry and Pedro had sponsored.

At home, Afonso proved generous to the point of absurdity. The tendency of kings in his time was to build royal absolutism, but he imperiled his own position and that of his son to follow by lavishly bestowing lands and concessions on noble friends without asking himself whether they would remain friends. His last major undertaking was to mix needlessly in a Castilian civil war by championing the claim to that throne of Juana la Beltraneja, illegitimate half-sister of Isabella the Catholic. After a defeat that cost both men and money, he realized that he was a political failure and retired from public life until his death in 1481.

JOHN II

Afonso's heir, John II (1481–1495), is known to the Portuguese as "The Perfect Prince," not in reference to personal virtue but to those traits of rulership Machiavelli admired in Cesare Borgia and Ferdinand of Aragon. His father's virtual abdication had made him effective ruler five years before his formal accession, but, though meaning to have a settlement with greater nobles who had gained semi-independence under the lax Afonso, he waited until his own coronation. The situation then required immediate action, because nobles headed by the current Duke of Bragança realized that the new king in no way resembled Afonso politically. A côrtes dominated by commoners complained of the laxity of royal administration regarding the nobility and the king ordered an investigation of the privileges formerly granted Bragança. During the search for documents at the duke's own estate, evidence was accidentally unearthed showing he was plotting with Isabel of Castile's husband, Ferdinand, for an invasion of Portugal and the overthrow of John. The king immediately arrested the powerful duke, placed him on trial, and confiscated his estates. Bragança was publicly beheaded at Évora in 1484, and several important nobles who had conspired with him were either imprisoned or fled the country.

The plotters had included young Diogo, Duke of Viseu, who was both John's cousin and the brother of his wife, Queen Leonor. The king told Viseu that he knew of his complicity but would spare him because of their relationship and the duke's youth. The latter seemed repentant, but within three months John learned that he was plotting with other leading nobles and a bishop to murder him and divide Portugal among themselves. The king summoned the young duke to his presence, and with three witnesses looking on, stabbed him to death. Again conspirators were run down; some were executed, some imprisoned never to emerge, and several forced into exile.[6]

These stern measures and the elimination of the greatest Portuguese nobles discouraged further plots. Neither John nor his immediate successors encountered much aristocratic opposition thereafter.

With a smooth-working absolutism at home, John could devote himself to his main self-appointed task of solving the riddle of Africa, superintending its circumnavigation, and establishing contact with India. John had greater means at his disposal than Prince Henry had possessed, for he was king as Henry had not been, and Portugal had meanwhile progressed in navigational skill. In place of the earlier oar-driven galleys there was now the Portuguese caravel, rounder and better suited to the Atlantic, moved entirely by lateen or square sails, and requiring a comparatively small crew. Although earlier progress had come in small spurts, John's seamen now were able to advance 1,000 additional miles per voyage.

Afonso V had lacked interest in discovery, yet it had continued during his reign. The crown had given private traders a monopoly of the commerce of Guinea, then a loose name for the west African coast, on condition that they make yearly advances in exploration. They had lived fairly well up to their bargain, and by the opening of John's reign had traced the shores of the lands today called Liberia, The Ivory Coast, Ghana, Togo, Dahomey, and Nigeria, and rounded the bend at the Bight of Biafra, beyond which Africa turns southward again.

John first ordered the construction of a fort on the Gold Coast, São Jorge da Mina (Elmina), to serve as a base for further expeditions southward and as a trading center to collect gold, ivory, pepper, and slaves from the nearby natives. His voyager, Diogo Cão, in two successive expeditions from 1482 to 1484, discovered the mouth of the Zaire (Congo) River and explored to Cape Cross in Southwest Africa, erecting stone pillars as tokens of possession at several coastal landmarks.

John believed himself on the verge of a great discovery, and in 1487 dispatched two expeditions, one for reconnaissance purposes to

6. For John's dealings with Bragança and Viseu, all modern accounts rest on Ruy de Pina's *Chronica d'El Rei Dom João II*, pp. 36–59.

India by the Mediterranean and Indian Ocean, and the other to round Africa if possible. The scouts were two Arabic-speaking Portuguese, Pero de Covilhâ and Afonso de Paiva, who proceeded first to Cairo, where they passed as Muslims. Later, at Aden, they separated, and Paiva set out for Abyssinia, considered the realm of Prester John. Covilhâ crossed to India, where he found Calicut in Malabar to be the main commercial center. Returning to Egypt, he found that Paiva had died, and, after further travels, went to explore Abyssinia himself. Before doing so, he sent from Cairo a letter to the king that presumably reached John and, in the light of later Portuguese procedure, it evidently stressed Calicut as the proper goal of expeditions by sea. Covilhâ reached Abyssinia, and nothing more was heard of him until 1520, when a Portuguese diplomatic expedition from India found him still living.[7]

Bartolomeu Dias commanded the fleet to round Africa, and he fulfilled his mission. He was blown past the southern extremity by heavy north winds and, turning eastward, sighted land at Mossel Bay, well beyond the Cape of Good Hope. He followed eastern Africa far enough to perceive that it bent northward, and then put back because his crews refused to sail further. On the return he rounded the great promontory that either he or the king named *Cabo da Boa Esperança* (Cape of Good Hope), "because it gave promise of the discovery of India so much hoped for and sought so many years." [8]

No more major discovery voyages occurred in John's reign. Dias reported that vessels heavier than caravels were needed to buffet the turbulent south Atlantic and was put to work superintending construction of rounder *naos*, or carracks, for the next expedition, intended to reach India. Meanwhile Christopher Columbus twice visited the West Indies for Castile, claiming the discovery of mainland Asia (Cuba) and Japan (Hispaniola). With Spain now in the discovery field, disputes arose that required over a year to adjust. Not until June 1494 did the Iberian kingdoms agree to the Treaty of Tordesillas, which, by an imaginary line from pole to pole, divided the Atlantic, and ultimately the non-Christian earth, between them.

John was only 40 in 1495, when he fell sick and died in October,

7. For the adventures of Covilhâ and Paiva, see Francisco Álvares, *The Prester John of the Indies*, II, 369–76.

8. João de Barros, *Asia*, p. 87.

of a disease thought to be dropsy. Malicious whisperers insinuated that the queen had poisoned him to make way for her brother Manuel, Duke of Beja, who did indeed succeed to the throne, because the royal couple's only son had died years earlier. There had been some estrangement between John and Leonor, but nothing known of her character suggests that she was a murderess.[9]

9. João Ameal, *Dona Leonor, "Princeza Perfeitissima,"* pp. 214–18.

6

The House of Beja

Sixteenth-century Portuguese considered Manuel I (1495–1521) inferior to John the Perfect and called him *O Venturoso*, or merely Fortunate. There seems no reason to question their judgment, for Manuel possessed neither the brain nor the ingenuity of his predecessor. He was fortunate in that he reaped the benefits and wealth of the discovery effort initiated by Princes Pedro and Henry and brought nearly to fruition by John II. To his credit, he displayed both energy and considerable judgment in selecting able men for his oriental conquests, though he often showed them less than gratitude. It cannot be said that he made wise use of most of the riches poured into his lap by his agents in the East, for he lavishly squandered much of what might have made the country prosperous. But regardless of the mistakes a wiser man might have avoided, his reign marked the high point of Portuguese history.

One of the charges hurled against Manuel is that of religious bigotry, as shown by his treatment of the Portuguese Jews. Jews had lived in the Iberian Peninsula since Roman times and had been accused, unjustly, of having aided in the Arab conquest. Under the Moors, they had been under only those disabilities common to all non-Muslims. In independent Portugal, they dwelt in segregated city quarters where they engaged in the money and banking occupations, generally without persecution. Their educational and literacy level was higher than that of the Christians and the government used them in civil service positions, though seldom in major offices. Many Jewish families had found it advantageous to accept baptism, and in some cases the fluid wealth of these "New Christians" made possible the marriage of their daughters into the highest noble families. Converted or not, the Jews were unpopular; the sincerity of Christian conversions remained always in doubt and preaching friars often stirred up the hatred of the Portuguese masses against them.

Portugal might have taken no action had not Spain led the way. Ferdinand and Isabella established the Inquisition in their kingdoms in 1477 and directed it mainly against converted Jews suspected of apostasy. In 1492 they ordered the expulsion of all Jews unwilling to become Christians and thousands left, some going to Portugal where John admitted them, though he exacted a stiff price.

Manuel came to the throne young and unmarried and sought the hand of Princess Isabella, daughter of the Spanish rulers, feeling that such a marriage might soon gain him the thrones of Aragon and Castile. The princess was as fierce a Jew-baiter as her parents and refused to marry him unless he converted or expelled them from Portugal. Manuel consulted the royal council but made the final decision himself: that all Jews and Muslims must be baptised or leave the country. The latter were generally allowed to go in peace; of the Jews, few actually left. There was no transportation available for most of them, and great numbers were seized, held, and baptised by force while they struggled and screamed. This virtually ended Judaism in Portugal, but the nation had gained superficial religious unity at a very heavy price. It was on the verge of becoming mistress of an overseas empire built on commerce, and now faced that experience deprived of the one class that could have given the empire some financial organization and solidity. A nation of landed gentry and peasants whose small middle class lacked large-scale financial experience proved unable to cope for long with the multifarious problems posed by its oriental empire.

MASTERY OF INDIA AND THE EAST

John II had made the preparations for the voyage to India and Manuel lost little time in carrying them out. Vasco da Gama, a Portuguese rural squire with seafaring experience, left the Tagus in

1497 with ships prepared by Bartolomeu Dias and probably with the information concerning Calicut that Covilhâ had sent to John. The voyage, most of it through unknown waters, was dangerous, yet within a year Gama had reached Calicut, where he negotiated with a Hindu ruler and obtained some spice cargo. By late summer of 1499 he was back in Lisbon with interesting information, as well as some misinformation, about East Africa and India. The returning voyagers thought India the source of the much-coveted spice, but the best of it came from the islands beyond Malacca. Several members of the expedition had entered a Hindu temple and, though bothered by the strange religious paintings and images they saw, took it for a Christian church and came away believing Calicut a Christian city.[1] Gama also gave the accurate but discouraging information that European goods had small appeal to Orientals.

The disheartening part of Gama's report and the meagerness of his cargo may have caused Manuel's government to ponder whether small Portugal should proceed with an oriental venture that might overstrain its slender manpower and resources. The decision was to persevere, and other voyages, discoveries, and ultimately conquests followed. Both Brazil and Madagascar were discovered by Pedro Álvares Cabral in 1500, and further knowledge was soon gained of eastern Africa and western India. Portuguese trading posts were established at several Indian points and ways found of overcoming the initial barriers to commerce. The hostility of Arabs and other Muslims who had hitherto dominated Indian Ocean commerce soon compelled the Portuguese to proceed to conquest. The two most noted conquistadors were Francisco de Almeida and Afonso de Albuquerque, who, in a single decade (1505–1515), made their country paramount in ocean supremacy. Almeida insured Portuguese naval supremacy when he defeated an Egyptian fleet off Diu in 1509; Albuquerque, with the aim of establishing Portuguese trade monopoly, nearly succeeded in sealing off the entrances and exits to the Indian Ocean. He captured Goa to serve as the center of Portuguese power and then took Malacca at the eastern end and Hormuz at the western end of the ocean. From Malacca he sent a fleet into the East Indies which discovered the Banda Islands and established indirect touch with the Moluccas. Albuquerque's one failure was at Aden, the key to the Red Sea, which he could not capture. Retention

1. Álvaro Velho? *Roteiro da Primeira Viagem de Vasco da Gama (1497–1499)*, p. 41.

of this port by the Muslims meant that oriental trade with Egypt and Europe could still pass by this route as it had done for so long in the past.

Portugal's eastern dominion was an empire of the seaways. In a sense it was no empire at all; at least when compared with the one built by Spain in America. Portugal had no desire to govern the teeming oriental millions; it wished only those coastal points strategically situated for the control of trade. Some subjugation of Asiatics did prove necessary, and then problems arose regarding the inevitable half-castes and the relations between the white and dark races. The best evidence seems to show that the Portuguese behaved as other Europeans have done in similar situations and treated the natives as inferiors.[2]

The Later Bejas

Manuel's first queen, Isabella, through whom he had hoped to unite the peninsula under his own rule, died after less than a year of marriage. It was the second wife, Maria, also Spanish, who became the mother of the next king, John III (1521–1557). The new monarch, who began ruling at the immature age of nineteen, was of average ability but scarcely more, and reigned at a crucial time. His small nation had overextended responsibilities and his treasury, though seemingly abounding in cash, had more demands upon it than could be met. Early in his reign, John unwisely dropped the advisors who had made Manuel's reign at least a partial success, but not all the decay of Portugal that began to be apparent could justly be laid at his door.

He was powerless to halt the heavy importation of African slaves, whose presence on the large estates caused the serious decline of the Portuguese farming peasantry. Nor could he prevent a falling-off of profits from his oriental dominions. Part of the decline was due to the heavy costs and losses involved in the maintenance of distant outposts; part was because of the expensive competition in trade existing as a result of Portugal's failure to close the Red Sea route. Much came because the Portuguese were inexperienced in large-scale business transactions and because Lisbon, though an ideal starting point for eastern voyages, was badly located for distribution through-

2. Charles R. Boxer, *The Portuguese Seaborne Empire, 1415–1825*, pp. 249–95.

out Europe of spices and other Asian luxuries. From almost the beginning, Antwerp showed signs of replacing Lisbon as a market center, and in time much eastern spice was barely halted at the Tagus before being shipped on to Antwerp. The empire did not wither in John's time, but it languished.

To John's credit was the continuance of Manuel's wise policy of neutrality in European affairs. Portugal joined no coalition and did not take part in any of the wars of the Reformation or Counter-Reformation in which Spain constantly participated in the sixteenth century. It had the most coveted overseas dominion of any European state and realized that a small country, with resources already taxed by holding and exploiting this, could not afford to strain them further.

Also on the credit side was the good sense John showed in bowing to financial necessity and abandoning several prestigious but expensive and useless Moroccan posts, two of them acquired by his father. Effective Portuguese colonization of Brazil began under government auspices in his reign, and this, ultimately, came to outweigh all else in importance.

The religious policy of John has received the most adverse criticism. He did not start as a religious bigot and perhaps never exactly became one, but he grew to believe all the dire stories told of the insincerity of converted Jews. To remedy what he believed to be a dangerous lack of national unity, as well as a threat to the purity of faith, he arranged in 1536 for the introduction of the Inquisition, along Castilian lines, into Portugal. Somewhat after his death it was established in the Portuguese East and, in a partial way, in Brazil.

The king, though poorly educated himself, was not altogether unfriendly to learning and the arts; his reign saw Portuguese humanism flourish in several fields. But as he became genuinely alarmed at the spread of Protestantism in Europe, he feared that heresy might infect Portugal. After inviting a number of distinguished foreign scholars to teach at Coimbra, he turned against them and permitted the Scottish humanist, George Buchanan (1506–1582), to be prosecuted and jailed for heresy. John then handed Coimbra and other teaching institutions over to the new Jesuit order, which, then at least, was the enemy of the humanism making a promising beginning in Portugal.

John fathered eleven children and outlived them all. His heir, therefore, was a grandson, Sebastian (1557–1578), a child of three who was left with no other preceptor than a great uncle, Cardinal

Henry. The aging churchman served as regent until the boy reached fourteen, when he assumed full powers. Sebastian was certainly not fit to exercise authority, as he proved to be wilful, conceited, and a religious fanatic, and indifferent to anything but his stubborn impulses. He was also subject to an unknown disease, which raised the suspicion that he might never be able to father children. In an era when teenage royal marriages were common, Sebastian remained celibate at twenty-four because his council wished to postpone his nuptials until he became stronger. So far as is known, the young king displayed no interest in women.

Sebastian wished to win military renown, to enlarge the Portuguese empire, and above all to be a crusader. The place he chose for the accomplishment of all three aims was Morocco, where his grandfather had relinquished several posts. Sebastian intended to recover these, besides bringing the whole country under his suzereignty.

He felt the opportunity had come in 1577 when a Moroccan civil war enabled him to ally with one faction. Stripping Portugal of men and money and leaving it without a suitable ruler should he fail to return, the headstrong youth invaded Morocco. Sebastian showed his greenness as a commander in the maneuvering that followed, and ended by leading the army into a trap at Alcazarquivir in 1578. The Portuguese were slaughtered; the foolish young ruler fell and was buried with some respect by the victorious Moors.

This catastrophe raised the whole question of the future of Portugal. For the moment Cardinal Henry, aged sixty-seven and suffering from tuberculosis, was king. The old celibate offered no prospect for continuance of the Beja dynasty; the real question was who was *his* heir? There were three possibilities, the likeliest being Philip II of Spain, whose grandfather had been Manuel I. The second was Catherina, Duchess of Bragança, related to the royal family but taken seriously by few people. The third was António, Prior of Crato, son of a royal prince but illegitimate, with the additional handicap that his mother had been Jewish. He might nevertheless have been the popular choice, but Philip's military strength enabled him to speak the deciding word when the time came.

The time came early in 1580 when Henry's expected death occurred. Following a few *pourparlers*, Philip moved an army into Portugal, which offered small resistance, though António tried to organize a defense. A côrtes at Tomar acclaimed Philip king, or rather was forced into accepting him. The Prior of Crato retired to the Azores where he maintained himself for a few years, but was then routed out by a Spanish expedition.

PORTUGUESE HUMANISM [3]

Portuguese literature was well developed by the time of the Renaissance, though in its earlier phases it had been rather imitative. Troubador songs from France and especially Provence had an echo in the Portuguese *cancioneiro*, devoted to love themes; often a species of palace poetry written for royalty and sometimes by royalty. The love verse of the *cancioneiro* reached a high development under Denís, himself a versifier. Denís was the grandson of Alfonso the Learned of Castile, whom he revered and emulated. Alfonso was a poet and Denís had poetic talent, though it is questionable whether all the 138 verses ascribed to him are his own work. After Denís, troubador poetry declined in Portugal and gave place to other forms.

The sixteenth-century Portuguese conquests in the East drew the attention of the ablest national historians to this epic, somewhat to the regrettable neglect of home affairs. The most noted was João de Barros (1496–1570), illegitimate but well educated, who had an official position that gave access to the documents he needed. Barros never went to the East, but his government standing enabled him to question numerous men returning from Asia, and no one has ever found his geographical knowledge inadequate. He is called the Portuguese Livy because he took the Roman historian as a model, though he surpasses Livy in accuracy. His work is entitled simply *Asia* and is divided into *décadas*, or decades, three of which were published in his lifetime and a fourth after his death, the total time span extending from Henry the Navigator to 1526. Nine more decades were later added by Diogo do Couto (1542–1616), who spent most of his adult life in the Orient.

Less famous than Barros, though scarcely his inferior as a historian, was Fernão Lopes de Castanheda (ca. 1500–1559), who had the advantage of having lived for ten years in India as a minor government clerk. In the preface to one of his volumes, Castanheda de-

3. The information in this section is drawn from Aubrey F. Bell, *Portuguese Literature*; Charles R. Boxer, *Three Historians of Portuguese Asia; Barros, Couto and Bocarro*; António José Saraiva, *História da Cultura em Portugal*, especially vol. II; Elizabeth Feist Hirsch, *Damião de Góis: The Life and Thought of a Portuguese Humanist, 1502–1574*; and Henry H. Hart, *Luis de Camöens and the Epic of the Lusiads*.

clared that he owed his accuracy to his long eastern residency, because only one who had seen the country could know whether the things said about it could have happened in the places indicated. On returning to Portugal without the wealth so many brought, Castanheda earned a living by menial labor while continuing the history begun at Goa. Much of his work, entitled *History of the Discovery and Conquest of India by the Portuguese*, was published before his death and portions translated into French and Italian. Castanheda lacked the pretentious style of Barros, yet comparison of their descriptions of the same events shows him sometimes the more effective of the two.

Damião de Góis (1502–1574), a man of many parts, is regarded as the foremost Portuguese humanist. He is remembered not for any one writing or any particular kind of writing but for his general erudition, culture, and standing as a man of the world. When young, he received an appointment as secretary to the Portuguese factory at Antwerp, which existed to distribute oriental products throughout Europe. From there he went with a diplomatic mission to Poland, and afterwards travelled through Holland, Germany, Denmark, Sweden, and Italy. At Wittenberg, he made a point of meeting the two arch heretics, Martin Luther and Philipp Melanchthon, and heard their views with no sign of shock. He was living in Louvain in 1542 when the French invaded the Low Countries, and was captured, taken to Paris, and held captive for nine months before being ransomed.

Góis was a music-lover and composer; when he returned to Lisbon the public was outraged at hearing from his house sounds of unfamiliar and undeniably foreign songs and instruments. Not surprisingly, this man who had eaten and drunk with heretics, and whose views were more heterodox than theirs, ran afoul of the Inquisition. He was arrested, frequently interrogated, and sentenced to incarceration and loss of property, though for some unexplained reason he was allowed to die a free man. Of his many writings, the best known is the *Chronicle of the Most Serene King Dom Manuel*, with whom, as a youth, he had been friendly. Published in a somewhat purged edition to placate enemies, this is a chronicle superior to older ones, but, taken by itself, does not show Góis as an outstanding historian because it lacks the broader sweep of the Barros and Castanheda works.

The greatest of all Portuguese literary figures was the epic poet Luís Vaz de Camões. He was born at either Lisbon or Coimbra in

1524 and attended the university at the latter city. He then moved to the capital, where he wrote copiously and fell in love, presumably more than once, although he never married. Camões had the bad fortune to offend John III, and left Portugal, going first as a soldier to Morocco where he lost an eye, and then to the East, where he remained for nearly twenty years. His adventures took him as far as China, where Portugal had recently leased the small Macao peninsula and where he resided with a Chinese mistress. He finally brought home none of the wealth gained by so many compatriots but instead the nearly completed manuscript of his immortal epic poem *Os Lusiadas* (The Lusitanians). He published it in 1572 with a dedication to young King Sebastian, who appears to have taken no interest in it. Camões lived until 1580, poor but in apparently not quite the starving condition tradition asserts.

Os Lusiadas, which is mainly a poetized account of Vasco da Gama's voyage to India and back, consists of ten cantos. Camões had made much the same voyage as Gama and so could describe in verse the scenes encountered by his heroes in Africa and Asia. At one point he has Vasco relate to an African prince the entire history of Portugal, or at least of its rulers, with great attention to the heart-rending story of Inés de Castro. The gods and goddesses of Olympus, under their Roman names, constantly play a part, either for or against the Portuguese, because Camões took the *Aeneid* of Vergil as his model. Venus is the especial protector of Gama, as she had been of Aeneas in the Latin epic.

A generation earlier, no one would have been disturbed by the part played by pagan deities in the poem, but the Inquisition had meanwhile appeared and Portugal was not the same as in Camões' carefree youth. Knowing that an ecclesiastical censor must be mollified, Camões slipped in a speech by Venus to the Lusitanians near the conclusion in which she reminds them that she and the other gods are only imaginary. If this little stratagem was really necessary, it worked, and there was no objection to publication by the Church.

7

Submergence and Reappearance

THE HAPSBURG SETTLEMENT

When Philip II of Hapsburg seized the Portuguese throne he promised a purely personal union that would leave his new kingdom as independent as before. He began with a long sojourn in Portugal, during which he guaranteed separation of the two governments and promised that the Portuguese language and laws should be used in the governance of the country. Moreover, there would be no Spanish encroachment on the overseas empire of Portugal. This all sounded well, but the Portuguese felt sceptical and time proved their misgivings well-founded. Philip, it must be said, was a man of his word, and for the rest of his reign lived up to the promises fairly well. But under his son and grandson the Portuguese received ample proof of an intention to incorporate them into Spain.

Inevitable difficulties arose at the very beginning. The Portuguese policy of isolation from European politics could not be continued, for now all the enemies of Spain became automatically Portugal's enemies. The colonial empire, both in the East and Brazil, which had enjoyed near immunity from attack, now became fair game for all. Portuguese submergence coincided in time with the determination of other Europeans, notably the Dutch, English, and French, to enter the overseas competition, which their internal situations had previously kept them from entering. The Portuguese empire, more vulnerable and less well guarded than Spain's, was attacked everywhere and a large part of it passed into foreign hands.

Portugal lost a considerable part of its naval strength in 1588 in the merging with Philip's great Armada against England, and suffered heavily in the ensuing disaster. The Spaniards could rebuild their fleet and within a decade were as powerful as ever on the sea; less attention was given to Portugal's fleet. When attacks were made on the Hapsburg overseas possessions, the Madrid statesmen naturally gave defensive priority to those of Spain.

As long as the original Spanish promises were reasonably well kept, the union actually had some economic value to Portugal. For years no demand was made for financial contributions to Madrid for purely Spanish affairs, and Portuguese merchants now had some access to the markets of the New World and made full use of these opportunities. The home Spanish economy was much larger than that of Portugal and gave opportunities for investment that the converted Jewish class, now beginning to emerge again, could and did exploit. But the Portuguese were not to be bought off with economic concessions; they knew themselves to be a conquered people. When the Spanish economy went into decline in the seventeenth century, Portuguese participation in the larger system became less advantageous as time passed.

Sebastianism

Although young Sebastian had fallen at the Battle of Alcazarquivir and been finally laid away at Ceuta, as anyone could easily learn, a considerable body of Portuguese opinion held that he still lived and would one day return to restore the glories of his people. Because so many desperately wished this to be true, the cult of *Sebastianismo* was born. It is not surprising, in view of the Portuguese national sadness, that pretenders began to appear. During the years when the vanished king could reasonably be living, the claimants needed to be of approximately the right age and, if possible, to resemble him in appearance. Ultimately the time passed when a purely physical Sebastian could still exist and the legend came to have a religious-mystical aspect, similar to the medieval German belief in the lengthy slumber of Frederick Barbarossa in the Kyffhäuser.

Of the pretenders who appeared in the twenty years following the death of Sebastian, the first was a Portuguese faker and mock hermit, the second a Portuguese monk, the third a Spanish soldier and pastry cook, and the fourth and last a Calabrian Italian. One by one they were taken by the Spanish authorities in Portugal or Italy, shown to be frauds, and in three cases executed and in the fourth sent as an oarsman to the galleys. The audacity of the Calabrian exceeded that of the others; not only had he no resemblance to the late king but he could not speak a word of Portuguese. Even the most gullible failed to be impressed by his assertion that he had taken a vow not to use his native tongue.

The cult of Sebastianism went on, however, and when the Bragança line restored Portuguese independence in 1640, the new king, John IV, had to agree that if Sebastian should reappear he would immediately surrender the throne to him. The departed ruler would then have been eighty-six years old. Among some Portuguese the return of a messianic Sebastian continued to be expected. "A foreigner traveling in Portugal in the early eighteenth century reported that half of the Portuguese were waiting for the messiah and the other half for Sebastian." [1] Just when Sebastianism finally vanished among the peasantry is impossible to say.

OVERSEAS LOSSES AND RECOVERIES

By the opening of the seventeenth century or shortly after, the Dutch had become the world's foremost naval power. They strove to gain an overseas empire, acting through their East and West India Companies, and had ambitions similar to Portugal's earlier ones. They had no wish for large land dominions but strove instead to control islands and seaports for profitable trade. During the first half of the century, they endeavored to gain for themselves much the same empire that Portugal had built and still held. Once they had learned to make the voyage around the Cape of Good Hope and across the Indian Ocean, as well as to reach the Orient via the Pacific, the Dutch rapidly dispossessed the Portuguese in many places. A generation after the end of Spanish-Hapsburg domination, Portugal's oriental holdings had been reduced to substantially those of the twentieth century. The country held on to the India posts and several east African ports, Macao in China, and half the island of Timor. Portugal

---

1. Mary Elizabeth Brooks, A *King for Portugal*, p. 49. By this reference to messianic hopes, the foreigner probably referred to the Judaistic ideas existing beneath the surface in Portugal.

could be somewhat reconciled to the losses, for the Orient had ceased to be as profitable as it had once been. The English took some prizes as well, although the principal one, Bombay, was gained later and peaceably.

In Brazil and the Atlantic, matters had a different conclusion. Before 1580, only a few Portuguese had migrated to Brazil; after that year emigration increased considerably, owing both to the unpopularity of the home administration and to the growing economic importance of the large colony. Hence, when the Dutch attacked Brazil in earnest in 1624, Portuguese numbers there were sufficient for an effective defense, although for a time the Hollanders appeared to have won. They held the Brazilian coast from the Amazon mouth almost to Baia, and it seemed but a question of time until they would take the rest. Their economic motive was to gain for themselves the profits from Brazilian sugar and control the importation of African slaves to Brazil. The principal source of slaves was Angola in western Africa, where Portugal had held several settlements since the previous century. The Dutch attempted to dominate this end of the traffic, and for a time did hold Luanda, the principal Angolan port. However, Portugal reacted vigorously, especially after the regaining of independence in 1640 had lifted national morale. The Dutch were expelled from Angola, and by 1654 the Portuguese had driven them from Brazil.[2] The growing importance of this huge colonial appendage during the seventeenth and eighteenth centuries, plus the African holdings and what was left in the Orient, made Portugal still one of the leading European overseas powers.

Independence Restored

The loss of some colonial possessions and foreign attacks on others put the Portuguese in a rebellious frame of mind, but it was a series of home circumstances that precipitated the final outbreak. After the death of Philip II (Philip I of Portugal), European Portugal fared badly and each reign saw some of the original guarantees whittled down or completely violated. Philip III of Spain, indolent and pleasure-loving, ignored Portugal as far as possible during the twenty-three years he reigned. He paid it only one visit, and preparatory to

2. Dutch effort to dominate the South Atlantic is described by Charles R. Boxer, *Salvador de Sá and the Struggle for Brazil and Angola, 1602–1686,* and *The Dutch in Brazil, 1624–1654.*

that collected a forced donation of money to put the royal palace at Lisbon in better shape for his reception. Philip allowed Spanish officials to replace Portuguese both at home and overseas, and once tried unsuccessfully to put a Spaniard in command of the Portuguese armed forces.

Philip IV of Spain came to the throne in 1621, and from the day of his accession had as minister the Count-Duke of Olivares, who became all-powerful as the years went by. Olivares' policy was to unify tightly the whole Iberian Peninsula, which meant wiping out not only the local institutions of Portugal but those of Aragon and Catalonia as well. Such a policy could never work, considering the stiff-necked character of the Iberian peoples, and stood less chance than ever now that Spain's most powerful years had passed and the country was visibly weakening.

Spain entered the Thirty Years War on the Catholic side in 1634, and Olivares began to seek new revenues in all possible places, including Portugal. One of his measures was the creation of a salt monopoly, which drew Portuguese protests, but these only caused him to tighten his grip on the vassal country. He appointed an energetic woman, Margaret of Mantua, Vicereine of Portugal because of her complete devotion to the Hapsburg interests. Attempts to collect new taxes caused riots to break out at Évora in 1637; these were brought under control with the aid of Spanish troops, and two fomenters escaped death by timely flight.

Leading men in Portugal now plotted secretly for national independence and the expulsion of the Hapsburgs. Their hopes for a king centered in John, Duke of Bragança, grandson of the Catherina who had been one of the claimants following the death of Cardinal Henry. For some time, however, Duke John refused to commit himself because he was timid and feared the consequences to himself in case the attempt failed. Repeated failures to arouse John's courage caused the conspirators' hopes to turn toward his brother, the more courageous Duarte, or, if he should not consent, toward the establishment of an aristocratic republic. It was finally John's Spanish wife, Luisa de Guzmán, with queenly aspirations, who persuaded John to take the risk.[3]

France and Spain were opponents in the Thirty Years War, and Cardinal Richelieu, minister of Louis XIII of France, saw a chance

---

3. Damião Peres, *Edição Monumental*, V, 280–81.

to weaken his enemy because of the known dissension in both Catalonia and Portugal. He sent an agent to Lisbon empowered to make
sweeping promises of French military aid and territorial aggrandize-
ment afterward, at Spanish expense, as a reward for rebelling. Olivares,
meanwhile, who distrusted Duke John's professed loyalty to Philip
IV, took what seemed a clever means of disposing of him. He appointed John governor of all Portuguese armed forces, designing the
appointment as a trap. Bragança, in his new capacity, would need
to travel about the country, and, while inspecting some fortress or
warship, could easily be abducted and taken to Spain. The duke saw
through this and, though accepting the appointment, took care never
to be in a vulnerable position or to travel without an armed escort.
Meanwhile, he allowed himself to be won over to the cause of national independence as the sole candidate for the throne.

The awaited moment came at the end of 1640. Revolt in Catalonia had broken out and reached serious proportions. Olivares issued
a series of orders ostensibly intended to move the entire Portuguese
fleet and thousands of soldiers to Spain to be incorporated into the
Hapsburg forces for suppression of the Catalan rebellion; in reality
to be sent wherever he might choose. Leading persons staged a well-
planned rising in Lisbon, timed when Spanish forces in Portugal were
at minimum strength. They easily overpowered the few sentinals
guarding public buildings and raised the cry: "Long live King Dom
John IV!" [4] Margaret of Mantua, though she argued vociferously,
was bluntly informed of her deposition. The city enthusiastically
welcomed the change and the *câmara* (municipal council) joyfully
acclaimed the new ruler. The rest of Portugal soon joined in, and, in
the absence of any force capable of suppressing the rising, the nation
was independent as of December 1640.

The House of Bragança, Portugal's last royal line, now com-
mencing its 270-year reign, differed in the manner of its accession
from that of John of Avís in 1385. The first John had been approved
by the côrtes of Coimbra before his formal enthronement, whereas
Bragança owed nothing to a côrtes and could maintain that he merely
resumed the Portuguese royal powers usurped by Spain. He thus
reconciled his irregular assumption of authority with the ideas of
kingly despotism current at the time.

4. *Ibid.*, p. 285. Underlying economic causes of the Portuguese revolt and
restoration are given by Vitorino Magalhães Godinho, *Ensaios*, II, 257–91.

8

A New Portugal

REORGANIZATION

Something more than the initial shouting was required to place the new monarchy firmly on its feet. A coronation was arranged for John IV of Bragança and Queen Luisa in Lisbon, during which a learned jurisconsult delivered a stirring patriotic address. Coimbra University provided a celebration lasting two months and consisting of both academic and religious exercises, interspersed with fireworks, equestrian exhibitions, and various games.[1]

After the tumult died down, John faced serious problems. The Spanish weakness that had permitted the recent *coup d'état* might be only temporary and the national defenses needed immediate bolstering. Some important Portuguese magnates and bishops had profited by the Spanish association and, though their voices had been drowned in the popular acclaim of John, they remained disaffected. Several noblemen immediately left for Spain, and Sebastião de Matos de Noronha, Archbishop of Braga, worked up a conspiracy to hand Portugal back to Philip IV.

The archbishop's plans failed primarily because too many entered into them. One conspirator betrayed the rest and informed John, who, however timid he had been as a duke, showed that he was a

---

1. Damião Peres, in *Edição Monumental*, VI, 11.

worthy king. He arrested many leading persons, including several important churchmen, and executed the principal noble plotters. Archbishop Matos died in prison, and a Bishop of Martíria spent his remaining years in the forced seclusion of a convent.[2]

Fortunately for Portugal, the Spanish military decline continued. In 1643, Philip's principal army suffered a crushing defeat by the French Duke d'Enghien at Rocroi in the Ardennes, with the loss of 15,000 men and all its standards and artillery. Rocroi did not altogether break Spain's military power, and within a few months Spanish troops partially redeemed their reputation. But the shortage of trained soldiers created by Rocroi and the need for coping with the Catalan revolt, besides a later one in Spanish-held Sicily, kept Philip IV from undertaking energetic military measures against Portugal.

The Bragança dynasty differed from the previous Beja one in its abandonment of the policy of isolation in European affairs, for John sought both allies and recognition of his government. He wished an alliance with France and the Netherlands against Spain, but the unhealthy state of European politics prevented the formation of such a coalition. Richelieu's fine promises proved to be meaningless; Portugal gained French and later Dutch recognition, but no more. England might ordinarily have helped, but its war between king and parliament was then breaking out. King Charles I recognized Portugal, but his own crown would soon drop from his severed head. John would gladly have had an alliance with Puritan parliament or Puritan Cromwell, but their preoccupation with other affairs prevented effective renewal of the Anglo-Portuguese pact until his son's time.

The papacy presented the thorniest problem of all, because the Popes during John's reign considered Philip of Spain their secular mainstay and would not offend him for a renascent Portugal that might prove short-lived. Not until 1659, a year after Spain had formally renounced all intention of reconquest, did Clement IX address Afonso VI as king.[3]

The Portuguese overseas possessions gladly acknowledged the new regime as fast as they learned of it. The only exception was Ceuta, held by a Spanish garrison, which continues to the present to be a possession of Spain.

2. *Ibid.*, pp. 14–19.
3. Ângelo Ribeiro, in *Edição Monumental*, VI, 23–24.

John lived and reigned until 1656 and with some ability saw the country through its trying period of rebirth. No one considered him brilliant, but he had shrewdness and common sense. Despite having been enthroned without benefit of côrtes, he summoned that body oftener than his Beja predecessors had customarily done, for in his initially vulnerable position he felt obliged to rely on all possible national support. In the delicate matter of money, he did not try to gain extra revenue without côrtes consent. He rebuilt some modest military strength and paid attention to the navy, for he was always in a state of war with Spain even when the conflict was dormant. John clearly realized that Portuguese mastery of the Indian Ocean was a thing of the past and that the colonial future lay in Brazil. His principal advisor, the Jesuit António Vieira, had been ordained to the priesthood in Brazil and much later died as a missionary there. At Vieira's urging, John chartered in 1649 the powerful Brazil Company with monopolistic privileges for supplying the colony with its most-needed commodities and the right to fix its own prices. The company received especial rights in Portugal, such as customs immunities and exemption of all invested capital from confiscation by the Inquisition.[4]

Bragança Family Problems

When John died, he left a kingdom in fair and improving condition. Its population, estimated at about 1.5 million, which had apparently been numerically static for generations, had begun to increase again. Portugal had some position in the world because it had been recognized by several European states. There had been an upsurge in agriculture and some revival of foreign commerce. Brazil remained a Crown possession and, moreover, was increasing greatly in size as intrepid frontiersmen there, called *Bandeirantes* (Banner Companies), carried out widespread explorations in the heart of South America.

An unfortunate element in the situation was John's son and successor Afonso VI (1656–1668), who almost from babyhood had shown that he could scarcely grow to be a normal man. At the age of two or three he had been attacked by what was called "malignant fever," which caused partial paralysis of his right side. He could

4. Charles R. Boxer, *The Portuguese Seaborne Empire, 1415–1825*, p. 222.

scarcely expectorate; he used his right hand only with difficulty, and distortion of one foot caused him to limp. It was impossible to avoid comparison between the new king and his brother Pedro, a good-looking boy of better than average ability.

Dowager Queen Luisa at first managed affairs, but in 1662 she had to hand over power completely to Afonso. There had meanwhile been arranged the marriage of the king's sister, Catherine of Bragança, to the newly enthroned Charles II of England. This renewal of an old alliance cost Portugal a heavy price. The dowry included Bombay and Tangier, which the English held for a time but ultimately abandoned. Afonso VI, or those acting in his name, included a cash sum of about £300,000 with the princess and gave English merchants trading privileges in Portugal and Portuguese India. In return, Portugal was guaranteed whatever protection England could afford against Spain and the right of Catherine to retain her Catholic faith in a Protestant country. Catherine went to England in 1662 and was married to Charles, to whom she bore no children and by whom, being far from beautiful, she was neglected. The English king, when dying, professed himself a Roman Catholic, and it is possible that Catherine had some influence in this decision.

Afonso VI virtually handed authority over to the Count of Castelo Melhor, who was the effective ruler for years. Those years brought an end to the war with Spain, which had made several minor invasions of Portugal, by a treaty that fully recognized the nation's independence. They also saw a marriage, celebrated but apparently never consummated, between Afonso and a French princess, Marie of Savoy. This young lady, of great beauty and ambition, understood the situation and was satisfied for a time to live with Afonso in a state of apparent matrimony. Prince Pedro, slightly younger than his sister-in-law, evidently fell in love with Marie at first sight. The two began working together to get rid of Castelo Melhor, whom Pedro particularly hated, and meanwhile keep Afonso amused with various pleasures. Pedro brought charges against the count of trying to have him poisoned and secured his banishment from court, though not from the country. Then, because they knew Afonso would recall Castelo Melhor at the first opportunity, Marie applied for an annulment of marriage on the grounds of the king's physical incompetence. After much consultation of physicians and much hearing of testimony, the queen won her case March 24, 1668; four days later she and Pedro were married.

A côrtes, summoned with the obvious thought that it would depose Afonso and make Pedro king, did not behave quite as anticipated. It agreed to accept the prince as heir and governor of the realm, but allowed Afonso to keep the royal title, which he bore in confinement until his death in 1683. Only then did Pedro become full-fledged King of Portugal, soon after which he became a widower, because Marie survived Afonso by only a few months. The one child of their union had been a daughter, destined to die young and unmarried. This placed Pedro under obligation to marry again to produce a male heir, and the situation called for haste because he was then about forty. He proved to be no matrimonial prize in the estimation of European courts, but after negotiating for several years for a bride, he finally obtained the daughter of the Elector Palatine of Neuburg, Maria Sophia. Wooed and won by proxy, she proved more prolific than the late Marie and bore six children, including John, the next ruler.

ECONOMICS, POLITICS, AND WAR

The legal reign of Pedro II (1683–1706) showed Portugal more prosperous than during its recent past. Population had grown and was estimated as over 2 million in 1700.[5] There was some expansion of domestic industry and increase of colonial trade. Indian commerce had become small, but the Brazilian fleets had grown enormously, with eighty-eight ships plying annually to Baia, Recife, Paraiba, and Rio de Janeiro. They brought home sugar in great quantities, tobacco, hides, and brazilwood yielding dyestuffs. Bandeirantes found gold deposits in São Paulo and the area subsequently known as Minas Gerais (General Mines), so after 1700, the Crown began to reap handsome revenues in gold.

Lisbon was a major European trade mart, and merchants of the leading foreign nations had communities there and in Oporto. The English enjoyed the most favored treatment, followed by the Dutch and French, the older foreign firms generally having contacts superior to the new ones. Religious services, if non-Catholic, could be performed only in the foreign legations and burials of heretics had to be conducted quietly and almost secretly. Minor trading establishments were maintained by the English at Viana do Castelo, Coim-

5. A. D. Francis, *The Methuens and Portugal, 1691–1708*, p. 13.

bra, and Faro. Foreign factors and merchants had little in common with the Portuguese upper classes, and for social life were primarily thrown upon their own devices.[6]

The War of the Grand Alliance, or Spanish Succession, began in 1701, because England, the Netherlands, and Austria refused to accept the deathbed decision of Charles II of Spain to will his throne and dominions to Philip, grandson of Louis XIV of France. They saw in this a disguised annexation of Spain and its great empire to France, and Louis, by imprudent remarks, increased their fears.

The English and Dutch were at first satisfied to have Portugal remain neutral, but then changed their minds and urged Pedro's government to enter the war. There followed a long period of bargaining, in which the allies offered Portugal territories they expected to conquer from Spain as inducement. Portugal agreed and signed a treaty in May 1703, accepting an alliance with Queen Anne of England, the States General of The Netherlands, and Emperor Leopold of Austria. Pedro bound himself to take an active part in the war and furnish a substantial army. The maritime powers, England and Holland, would use their navies to protect the coasts of Portugal and its overseas possessions. Archduke Charles of Austria, Hapsburg claimant of the Spanish throne, was expected soon to land in Portugal preparatory to invading Spain, and Pedro agreed to help him in every possible way.[7]

At the end of 1703 a special commercial treaty was signed in Lisbon between John Methuen, English Minister to Portugal, and the Marquis of Alegrete, Pedro's Councillor of State. The original text, in Latin, stipulated that English woollen manufactures should be admitted to Portugal and that, in return, Portuguese wines could be exported to England on more favorable terms than French wines.[8] Each side later claimed that the other had gained the better of the bargain but, because England obtained a needed wool market and Portugal could now undercut French wines in English sales, both parties apparently gained what they most wanted. Great Britain thenceforth held the upper hand in Portuguese trade, but such hegemony was sure to go somewhere in view of the nonindustrial

6. *Ibid.*, pp. 19–21.
7. Armando Marques Guedes, A *Aliança Inglêsa* (*Notas de História Diplomática*) 1383–1943, pp. 305–8.
8. An English translation of the Latin text is furnished by Francis, *The Methuens*, p. 198.

condition of Portugal. Portuguese viniculture gained a great stimulus, because hitherto barren districts of the Douro Valley could now be planted with grapes producing the heavy, sweet port wine.

Although the question of the Spanish throne had caused the war, the greater battles between France and the allies took place in Germany and along the Franco-Belgian frontier, and the Iberian part became a side issue.[9] Archduke Charles landed in Lisbon in 1704, but proved unable to mount a serious invasion of Spain, where Philip was already installed as king and generally accepted. An English fleet meanwhile captured Gibraltar, which a combined French-Spanish army failed to retake.

Charles then shifted operations to Catalonia, and, with English help, took Barcelona, which the allies held for several years. An invasion from the west by the Portuguese Marquis of Minas saw the capture of Salamanca, and on July 5, 1706, the advance guard of Portuguese cavalry dashed into Madrid, where Archduke Charles, though not present, was proclaimed king of Spain. The tide of the war then turned, because the general will of the Spaniards was to accept Philip of Bourbon as ruler and thus prevent the partition of their world empire among the allied states. Philip's commander, James, Duke of Berwick, forced the Portuguese out of Madrid and in 1707 defeated them and their Anglo-Dutch allies at Almansa near Valencia. Remnants of the beaten army retired to Catalonia, while Minas, with a shattered reputation, returned to Portugal. Following this, the Portuguese confined operations to small, indecisive frontier campaigns.

The war ended with a series of treaties in 1713, known collectively as the Peace of Utrecht, which left Philip in possession of the Spanish throne. Portugal terminated its war with France in that year, but peace with Spain did not come until 1715. By the time they signed the Treaty of Madrid, the Portuguese realized they could expect very little. They held a few places inside the Spanish frontier and agreed to abandon these in return for full rights to disputed Colônia do Sacramento in Uruguay and possession of the Amazon River mouth.

9. The Iberian side of the War of the Spanish Succession is covered by Damião Peres in *Edição Monumental*, VI, 134–78. Henry Kamen's account, in *The War of Succession in Spain, 1700–15*, concerns the diplomatic and economic aspects rather than the military. Nowhere is the military side concisely covered better than by R. Ernest and Trevor N. Dupuy in *Encyclopedia of Military History*, pp. 625–27.

9

The Eighteenth Century

Curious John V

Pedro II died in 1706 at the height of the war, and John V (1706–1750) succeeded him at the age of sixteen. "With D. John V pure absolutism installed itself on the Portuguese throne." [1] The inspiration came from France, where Louis XIV, "*Le roi soleil*" because of his splendor and power, had been the envy and model of European sovereigns from kings to the pettiest princes. With new sources of wealth, John became a passable Portuguese imitation of the mighty monarch of Versailles. The new king resembled his French exemplar in two important respects; he was superstitiously religious and possessed some capacity for hard work. Voltaire, his contemporary, made a typically Voltairian remark concerning him: "The monarch's gaieties were religious processions; when he took to building he built monasteries, and when he wanted a mistress, he chose a nun." [2] John had a more flattering way of describing himself; he claimed to be the monarch who "neither owed nor feared." His father had used the côrtes in his climb to the throne, but John felt no need for this body and never summoned it.

1. Ângelo Ribeiro, in *Edição Monumental*, VI, 179.
2. Quoted by Marcus Cheke, *Dictator of Portugal: a Life of the Marquis of Pombal*, 1699–1782, p. 8.

One of his first acts was to proclaim complete adherence to his allies in the war against France and Spain. He adhered loyally and nearly came to regret it, because in the end the greater powers signed their own treaties and obliged him to get the best terms he could with Spain.

The reign was peaceful except at the beginning and during the years 1716–1717, when the Portuguese fleet, recently somewhat re-modelled, entered the Mediterranean to aid Venice, whose holdings were being threatened by the Turks. In 1717 it fought the last major engagement in its history and defeated a Turkish fleet off Cape Mata-pan, close to the area where the British nearly finished the Italian navy in 1941. The victory produced no result, and the fleet came home leaving the Turks still in substantial possession of the eastern Mediterranean.

Voltaire was right in characterizing John's piety, for his education had been by Jesuit priests and devout women. Yet he did not lack intellectual tastes, one proof being the creation, under his auspices, of the Royal Academy of Portuguese History in 1720. By the close of the reign, this had produced many volumes of scholarly merit. John liked to attend its learned sessions, and he caused to be built the beautiful library of Coimbra University. He appreciated music, particularly if religious; he was fond of the opera and oversaw the creation of a royal choir for the palace chapel. To any objection that all this was but the pastime of a dilettante king, with no real roots in the country, the answer is that the prestige of the royal court was the prestige of the nation. John was following the fashion of his time, when all rulers, the Russian Czar included, liked to adorn their courts with evidences of learning and the fine arts. But it was not imitative zeal alone that moved him, and there is no reason to call his devotion to culture insincere.

Fortunately for his expensive tastes, John usually possessed the means to gratify them. During his reign, especially in the early part, gold revenue continued to pour in from Brazil, and when this some-what slackened, diamond deposits discovered there kept the colony a source of wealth. Portuguese emigrants, attracted by gold and other inducements, went in growing numbers to the huge South American dependency. Yet royal revenue fell off in the closing years of John's reign, and he bequeathed a load of debt to his successor.

For all his piety, John did not hesitate to oppose and even break relations with the papacy when he considered his prestige involved.

Until his time, the Pope's *nuncio* at Lisbon had borne a lower rank than cardinal, which seemed a slight to national honor, inasmuch as such dignitaries represented the papacy at Madrid, Paris, and Vienna. When the Pope twice rebuffed John's request for a cardinal's hat for the Lisbon nuncio, the king not only recalled his envoy from Rome but ordered all papal vassals expelled from Portuguese dominions. The deadlocked situation lasted two years, until 1730, when John finally had his way and obtained a cardinal as nuncio. Relations with Rome then so far improved that before John died he received for himself and all his successors the title "Most Faithful King" from Pope Benedict XIV.

John died in 1750 at the age of sixty-one. "The model always present in his mind was Louis XIV, of whom he said that '*nobody but he knew how to be a king.*' " [3] The deceased monarch had four legitimate children, including his successor, José, and an uncertain number of bastards by various mistresses, who included a nun.

POMBAL

José (1750–1777), the only one of his name to rule Portugal, has been likened to a late Merovingian monarch because he was a do-nothing who handed government over to an all-powerful deputy. Recent investigation shows that José was not altogether the cipher he seemed, but the effective ruler of Portugal in his reign was Sebastião de Carvalho e Melo (1699–1782), who received late in life the title Marquis of Pombal, by which he is remembered. One reason for the royal lassitude may have been that John had allowed José no part in state affairs, so that at thirty-six he was as new to kingly responsibilities as a teenage boy.

Pombal had reached the age of fifty-one by the opening of the new reign, and had had a diplomatic career of no great distinction in London and in Vienna, where he had married a daughter of the noted soldier Leopold von Daun. He returned to Lisbon just before John's death and became Minister for Foreign Affairs and War in the new ruler's cabinet. He arranged for payment of the late king's debts and began to dominate his colleagues, whom he excelled in ability. A boundary adjustment with Spain in South America led to an Indian outbreak, believed by Pombal to have been instigated by the Jesuit Order. Here began his hatred of the Jesuits, not evident

3. Ribeiro, *Edição Monumental*, VI, 191.

previously, that ended with his expulsion of the Company of Jesus from all Portuguese dominions.

The Lisbon earthquake of November 1, 1755, brought Pombal to full power and confirmed him in it for over two decades. The quake came in three separate shocks, lasting a total of about ten minutes. During the first, buildings collapsed, people were crushed to death, vehicles were overturned in the streets, and whole blocks of houses fell. The second tremor proved even more violent and caused the fall of buildings weakened by the first shock. The third did further damage to a city two-thirds of which already lay in ruins. Water from the Tagus poured into the lower parts of Lisbon, and elsewhere fires began consuming whatever was flammable. Deaths are estimated at 10,000 to 15,000, though, because the total population was not known and parish records were destroyed, the figures may be exaggerated. Terrified survivors fled the city, while criminals and the poorest elements seized the opportunity for plunder.[4]

The royal family did not suffer because it happened to be at the Belem villa, which escaped disaster. King José proved irresolute and is reported to have nervously asked those about him what could be done. The doubtless apocryphal reply, attributed to both the Marquis of Alorna and Pombal himself, is given as: "Bury the dead, care for the living, and close the harbors." Closure of the ports would seem to be a strange means of coping with disaster, and a modern Portuguese historian writes: "This banality was not of a kind to be applauded as an able program of government."[5]

Pombal acted vigorously in the emergency; several other ministers proved useless and one merely fled the scene. He nonetheless had staunch helpers among the nobles and officials, and the people in general behaved well. Pombal arranged relief measures, improvised hospitals, and organized volunteer companies to prevent thievery. Through his energy order was restored, and arrangements were made to bring all available food to Lisbon. The governments of Great Britain, France, and Spain sent or offered help, but Lisbon reemerged through the efforts of the Portuguese and mainly though those of Pombal.

Architects and engineers planned a new city, and Pombal saw to it that their plans were put in effect, though reconstruction re-

4. For information about the great quake and its aftermath, see T. D. Kendrick, *The Lisbon Earthquake*.
5. Ribeiro, *Edição Monumental*, VI, 203.

quired years and continued long after his time. Pombal's career has been variously and often unfavorably appraised, but for the rebuilding of their capital his countrymen owe him a debt of gratitude.

One aftermath of the quake hardened his anti-Jesuitical attitude. He and most educated men understood the disaster to be a purely natural phenomenon with no religious significance. But pamphleteers and preachers wildly declared it to be God's punishment of a people grown impious. Various religious orders took part in these tirades, but one half-crazed Jesuit agitator outdid the rest. Considering himself the principal target of accusations of impiety, Pombal, who had several private counts against the Jesuits, resolved to have a reckoning with the entire company at the first convenient moment.

The chance came in 1758 when an attempt was made to assassinate the king as he returned in his coach from a nocturnal assignation with a young married lady of the nobility. The attackers were presumably the husband and male in-laws of the Marchioness of Távora, the woman involved, along with other nobles. Because all the suspected parties were known opponents of Pombal, now virtually a dictator, he imprisoned them and put several to death.

During the Távora investigation, evidence was unearthed that Pombal interpreted as meaning Jesuit participation in the plot against José's life. At most, this testimony could have involved only one or two fanatical Jesuits, but the minister took the energetic steps he had planned for years. He persuaded the conventionally pious king in 1759 to sign a decree banishing every Jesuit from Portugal and its overseas possessions. He enforced the order with full rigor, and the Jesuits did not return to the country until the next century. This is the action for which Pombal is chiefly remembered; the one that causes his memory to be cursed or revered, as the individual chooses, after two centuries. In taking the drastic step, he had more than the Jesuits in mind, for he wished to subordinate the Portuguese clergy to the state, which he could best do by expelling his principal clerical antagonists. He had started a trend in Europe, because France and Spain banished the Jesuits within a decade and the Pope suppressed them altogether in 1773. Needless to say, this policy was later reversed, and the Jesuits, who preserved an underground organization until 1814, were then allowed to resume their functions openly.

Pombal was an economic as well as a political dictator. He strove to increase Portuguese industry, principally to prevent the financial drain caused by the nation's dependence on foreign imports. Although not basically anti-British, he tried, for the most part vainly, to break the English economic hold on his country, which had been felt even before the Methuen-Alegrete Treaty. His general solution to economic problems, both at home and in Brazil, was to place industry and commerce in the hands of large monopolistic companies, at the expense of small traders.[6]

Pombal held power until José's death in 1777. He received the title of marquis, by which he is known, only in 1770, for he was not of the genuine nobility. For all his selfishness and love of power, he made some attempt to modernize Portugal, a task too great for one individual in a single generation; therefore much of his work did not survive him long. During his last years of power, his regime became a sodden tyranny, often of a terrorist sort. As he aged, he grew less efficient but held authority stubbornly, and the king had grown so dependent upon him that he resisted all pleas to turn against the redoubtable old man.

José's successor, Maria I (1777–1816), was a woman of more than average superstitious piety who had let it be known that, with her accession, the influence and possibly the life of Pombal would end. Maria's hatred of him came partly from religious reasons and partly from resentment of his influence over her father. She had the Távoras posthumously vindicated and commenced a legal proceeding against Pombal, who was meanwhile banished to his country estate. The old minister was adjudged guilty of many crimes, but the queen finally spared him the punishment she declared he deserved because of his advanced age. He obliged her by dying in 1782 at the age of eighty-three. Except for a modernized Lisbon and the absence of Jesuits, Portuguese conditions became substantially what they had been before his time.

FIN DE SIÈCLE

The priesthood still dominated Portugal, yet a few changes had come after all. Freemasonry had entered the country during the 1730s and had later spread, in spite of attempts by the Church and the authorities to suppress it. Masonic membership was not then absolutely incompatible with Catholic faith, but it did imply anti-

6. See Jorge de Macedo, "Marques de Pombal," Os Grandes Portugueses, II, 141–52, and his A Situação Económica no Tempo de Pombal, both especially concerning Pombal's economic policies.

clericalism. Masonry had come primarily from England, and on at least one occasion Lisbon initiates met on board an English warship.[7] Junior officers of the army seemed especially susceptible to it, and Coimbra, the university city, had a lodge including both faculty and students.

Portuguese science, which had made a promising beginning in the sixteenth century, had nearly vanished by the eighteenth. Ignorance was not confined to the poor, for the nobility was scarcely more enlightened; the average nobleman's education consisted largely of obscurantist religious doctrine. He shared with his peasants an enthusiasm for bullfights and miracles. The major differences seemed to be the clothes they wore and the artistocrat's ability better to satisfy his often great capacity for eating.

José's failure to beget a son had caused him to solve the succession problem by wedding his heiress, Maria, to her uncle, his brother, Pedro. Pedro, married to the queen, bore the courtesy title El-Rei and is remembered as Pedro III. There is little to say of this pair, who produced a succession of children including the one who became John VI. Pedro himself was a pious nonentity, chiefly concerned with prayers and masses, and when he died in 1786, his widowed niece mourned him extravagantly. Maria, originally a woman of some determination, began to fail mentally after his death, and by 1792 was patently unfit to govern. Her eldest living son, John, took charge of state affairs and in 1799 was formally declared Prince-Regent. By then Europe had entered the troubled times of the French Revolution, from which Portugal could not hope to emerge unscathed.

7. Cheke, *Carlota Joaquina, Queen of Portugal,* p. 13.

10

Invasion, Exile, and War

First Impacts

For several years after the storming of the Bastille by a French mob on July 14, 1789, Portugal lay wrapped in the slumber Pombal's downfall had restored. It was fairly remote from the scene; no one yet appreciated the importance of the event, and the enduring British alliance seemed a guarantee of safety.

Appearances changed in 1793 when Republican France, after dethroning Louis XVI and Marie Antoinette, sent them to the guillotine. It was easy to see the importance of this, and Portugal joined the First Coalition, headed by Great Britain, against France. France soon began to win, as it conquered Holland and obliged Prussia and Spain to sign separate peace treaties. Next, through the brilliance of young General Bonaparte, it knocked Sardinia and Austria out of the war and overran northern Italy. Britain and Portugal remained unconquered; the former because of its insular position and the latter because of its failure to stand high on the French agenda of conquest. Portugal, meanwhile, proved genuinely helpful to England, as its ports were convenient for sustaining the British fleets based on Gibraltar.

In 1799, Bonaparte overthrew the French Directory and became First Consul, meaning dictator, of France. He now had the decrepit Spanish Bourbon monarchy as an uncomfortable ally; that monarchy was dominated by the queen's ambitious favorite, Manuel de Godoy, and the Spaniards had never quite given up hope of reannexing Portugal. Prodded by Bonaparte, Godoy issued an ultimatum in 1801 to the Prince Regent, demanding immediate termination of the British connection, an alliance with Spain, an indemnity, and the surrender of some territory. As the prince vacillated, the Spaniards invaded both northern and southern Portugal, while a French force stood by ready to help. The allies did not then press matters to the limit, however, because Bonaparte was about to conclude the Peace of Amiens with England that brought the war to a temporary halt. The Spaniards evacuated Portugal but retained the Olivença district in the Alto Alentejo east of the Guadiana River. This is the only European territory ever lost by Portugal, for Spain still retained it at the close of the Napoleonic era.[1]

The Bragança Decampment

Portugal was only temporarily spared. The Peace of Amiens lasted only fifteen months, and in May 1803 France and England again went to war. Late in the following year, after a plebiscite that appeared to show a French wish for monarchy, Bonaparte crowned himself Napoleon, Emperor of the French. With Spain soon again an ally, he once more faced Europe, and during 1805, 1806, and 1807 proceeded to crush Austria, virtually annihilate Prussia, and make a cordial, if ephemeral alliance with Russian Czar Alexander I after defeating him in battle. He stood at his peak of success, with England again his sole remaining powerful adversary. To force the British to their knees economically, he proclaimed the Continental System, whereby all European countries under his influence would help ruin English commerce by excluding it from their ports. This was sure to bring Portugal importantly into the picture, because this policy proved understandably unpopular in Europe and Portuguese harbors furnished entrances through which British goods could pass.

Prince-Regent John had meanwhile governed in a rather lackadaisical way for his mother. Time would show him as being far from a fool, but he looked like one on first sight—being short, round, and clumsily built, with bad manners, and possessing a fat, stupid face, protruding eyes, thick lips, and a half-open mouth. His wife Carlota

1. The outstanding authority on this territorial loss is J. M. de Queiroz Velloso, *Como perdemos Olivença*.

Joaquina, daughter of Charles IV of Spain, was a hideously ugly woman with a sour disposition.[2] This extremely unattractive pair had produced several children, of whom the two most important were Pedro and Miguel, the first a future emperor of Brazil and the second a king of Portugal. John and Carlota had become *esposos desavindos* (disagreeing spouses), an expression really too soft for the hatred they bore each other. Carlota had the greater capacity for hatred; she had already tried to have her husband declared insane and had written urging her royal Spanish father to invade Portugal and place her in total charge.

Napoleon exploded a diplomatic bombshell in August 1807 when his government and that of Spain presented a joint ultimatum in Lisbon demanding the closure of all Portuguese ports to the English and the arrest of all British subjects in the country, with confiscation of their property. John, who usually vacillated in an emergency, rather did so now, but did resist the demand for the arrest of the Englishmen. An invasion clearly impended, and while some of the prince's advisors urged compliance with the ultimatum, others advocated what had more than once been suggested in past times of danger— namely, removal of the royal family to Brazil. John hesitated and Andoche Junot, with a small French army from Spain, crossed the frontier and began a march on Lisbon. The capital was in a terrified state and looked to its rulers for a decision—any decision—in this crisis, but looked in vain. Carlota Joaquina thought of leaving John and taking refuge in Spain, and wrote asking her parents to shelter her and the Bragança daughters.

Junot's invasion was in reality less formidable than it must have seemed. He led but a small, poorly equipped army, consisting mostly of raw recruits, many of them under military age. With any leadership and courage, the Portuguese could easily have thrown back the French, but the spell of Napoleon was strong. Portugal thought not in terms of the approaching green levies but of the magnificent troops who had triumphed recently at Ulm, Austerlitz, Jena, Auerstadt, and Friedland.

The English ambassador, Lord Strangford, urged the Bragança prince to go to Brazil, promising the protection of the British Navy during the long voyage and his country's full collaboration in the eventual expulsion of the French. A fleet from England had arrived and stood ready in the Tagus, either to convoy the royal fugitives or

2. Marcus Cheke, *Carlota Joaquina*, pp. 4, 8.

blockade the city, depending on what John decided to do. There was also an ample Portuguese squadron at hand, containing space enough to bear the Braganças and followers to Brazil.

At the last possible moment, with Junot's advance guard nearly at hand, the Prince-Regent loaded his family, including demented old Queen Maria, in the ships and embarked for Brazil. Thousands of courtiers and camp followers, as well as several military units, accompanied the Braganças, and a considerable treasure was also taken.

Crossing the bar of the Tagus, the fleet and its royal cargo commenced a very unpleasant voyage to the Southern Hemisphere— unpleasant because of lack of accommodations for delicately nurtured passengers.[3] There had been no adequate preparation of baggage, and Prince John is reported to have embarked without a change of underwear, which, considering his aversion to bathing, may have bothered him less than it did those about him. The Bragança flight proved a boon to Brazil, but for the sake of his prestige at home, John would have been well advised to go no farther than the Azores or Madeiras.

Brazil was reached in safety and Rio de Janeiro became, for thirteen years, the capital of the Portuguese empire. Lord Strangford and other diplomats from friendly states transferred to Rio, and nobles who had accompanied John found homes in the city, sometimes to the inconvenience of colonial inhabitants. John soon learned to like Brazil, and by a series of wise laws made himself popular in his new home.

Junot meanwhile marched unopposed into Lisbon, and Portuguese outside the capital gradually learned that their rulers had decamped, apparently leaving them to their own devices. The Braganças had abandoned Portugal; the next move was up to its people.

PENINSULAR WAR

Junot, in possession of Lisbon, assured the people by proclamation that he came to liberate them from the British. He then formed 9,000 men of the Portuguese army into a "Portuguese Legion" and sent it to France to fight Napoleon's battles. He confiscated the properties of those who had accompanied the Prince-Regent to Brazil

3. Tobias Monteiro, *História do Imperio: A Elaboração da Independencia*, p. 59. Because of unsanitary shipboard conditions and the abundance of lice, the women cut their hair short, which, on arrival at Rio, started a fashion among Brazilian ladies.

and levied a cash contribution on the country. The upper classes seemed to accept the French usurpation, but the commoners gave many signs of unrest.

Although Spain had acted as Napoleon's ally, its turn came next. Early in 1808, the Emperor declared the Spanish royal family deposed and his brother, Joseph Bonaparte, King of Spain. Riots in Madrid on May 2, 1808, though suppressed with slaughter by the French, gave the signal for a general national revolt.[4] Junot was obliged to send part of his army to cope with the Spanish situation; Spanish troops, who had taken some subordinate role in the occupation of Portugal, now changed sides or were disarmed by the French. The British ministry, which had awaited an opportunity to strike Napoleon in a vulnerable spot, sent General Sir Arthur Wellesley to the peninsula to aid the Portuguese and Spaniards. Wellesley landed at Mondego Bay and advanced on Lisbon. With the help of a Portuguese division he defeated the French at Roliça and Vimeiro, after which Junot agreed to evacuate his troops from Portugal in British ships. The English force had to protect the departing French from Portuguese retaliation because of the atrocities they had committed.

Portugal was thus free of Napoleon's forces by September 1808, but the Emperor would certainly not accept this defeat without a serious attempt to retrieve prestige. A council of regency now governed the country in the name of the absent John and Maria, and English General William Carr Beresford was made responsible for whipping the Portuguese army into shape. It was at first found to be slovenly and indolent, but under Beresford's tutelage it improved until one British officer declared the men "excellent troops equal to contend with the French infantry; under *ordinary circumstances* acting with the bravery of their island allies." [5]

Napoleon took the field in person with overwhelming force late in 1808, but confined his effort to Spain, from which he retired early the next year because of a new war with Austria. Soon after this, Marshal Nicolas Soult invaded north Portugal from Spain and took and sacked Oporto, but was driven out by Wellesley, aided by a now comparatively disciplined Portuguese army. Wellesley then led an Anglo-Portuguese expedition into Spain in 1809. He penetrated nearly to Madrid and defeated French Marshal Claude Victor at Talavera

4. There are many first-hand accounts of the Madrid rising, but the paintings of Goya illustrate it best.
5. Michael Glover, *Wellington's Peninsular Victories*, p. 24.

de la Reina on the Tagus. But the victory was little better than a draw, and the superior French forces in Spain began converging upon him, so Wellesley retired to Portugal. He realized that there would soon be a massive thrust into that country, unquestionably toward Lisbon, and that all soldiers and available laborers would be needed to prepare the defenses.

Lisbon lies near the end of a peninsula formed by the Atlantic and the wide mouth of the Tagus. At Tôrres Vedras, Sobral, and the capital itself, Wellesley had thousands of palisades and *fascines* (bound bundles of wood) constructed. He set up three lines of fortifications, confident that the French, who lived off an invaded country and consequently must remain mobile, could not force these well-defended barriers and would have to retreat. For this work, thousands of conscripted Portuguese peasants and laborers were used. The law of the country made every able-bodied man liable for service in the militia or the *ordenança* (labor battalion). Such conscripts could not do much fighting, but they could dig, and Wellesley, who meanwhile had been created Viscount Wellington of Talavera, used them effectively to prepare fortifications.

Napoleon, always dissatisfied with his subordinates' performance in the peninsula, changed marshals frequently, and the one now chosen to lose a reputation in Portugal was André Massena, hitherto very successful. Wellington, having completed the fortifications and aware that Massena would depend on Portugal for food, laid waste much of the region through which he would have to pass and, by the destruction of bridges, created many physical obstacles.

Massena began his advance from Valladolid on May 10, 1810, with a far larger army than Wellington could muster. The viscount had no thought of risking everything on a battle outside the Tôrres Vedras lines, but did repel a fierce assault by three French corps at Buçaco with heavy loss. Wellington retired without pursuit to the lines, and as Massena advanced his food problem grew. He reached the fortifications, only to encounter Wellington with a well-fed army defending them, and for some time maneuvered without launching an attack. He thought of extending operations below the Tagus and ordered a bridge constructed at Santarem, but was told by his engineers that this was an impossible project. He started a general retreat on the night of November 14, intending to retire secretly, and conducted the first stage so expertly that Wellington could not immediately mount a pursuit. The French committed atrocities against the population as they retired, and the Portuguese repaid them in kind whenever possible. An order by Napoleon reached Massena in February 1811 to the effect that he should unite with Marshal Soult, then operating in southern Spain, and resume the offensive, but this had become physically impossible. Massena could only continue the retreat, harassed and worn down by Wellington and *guerrilhas* of the Portuguese countryside. At several points he tried to make a stand, but ended by abandoning all positions. By the time his army staggered into Ciudad Rodrigo in Spain, its total loss had mounted to 25,000; Wellington's was something like 4,000.

The Peninsular War lasted three years longer, but did not seriously involve Portugal after Massena's disastrous retreat. Wellington, ultimately a duke, kept his Portuguese troops during the remaining Spanish campaigns and his final invasion of France. He had Spanish contingents, but he and Beresford, in the later battles, preferred to use the Portuguese they had disciplined themselves.[6] The war ended, apparently for good, when Napoleon abdicated in April 1814 and was sent to Elba. There followed, of course, the aftermath of the Hundred Days and Waterloo, but this was over too soon to affect Portugal.

6. The complete Portuguese side of the Peninsular War is covered by Lopes de Almeida, *Edição Monumental*, VI, 321–60. The British side is handled ably by Elizabeth Longford, *Wellington: The Years of the Sword*.

11

Miguel, Pedro, and the Constitution

THE CONGRESS OF VIENNA

The Portuguese delegation at the Congress of Vienna in 1814–1815 was headed by the Count of Palmela (1781–1850), who came with instructions from the Prince-Regent at Rio. The major powers dominated the congress and Portugal had little interest in most of their European deliberations. Palmela desired adjustment of the boundary between Brazil and French Guiana on Portugal's terms, recovery of Olivença from Spain, Portuguese exemption from a general treaty abolishing slavery, abrogation of a recent treaty with Great Britain considered disadvantageous to Portugal, and some war indemnity from France. He obtained part of what he sought; the South American boundary adjustment was arranged, the British consented to a new treaty, and Palmela gained a promise of a French indemnity. Portugal refused the abolition treaty, though agreeing to stop the Brazilian slave traffic, the loss of which meant difficulties for the Brazilian planters. The great powers recognized the justice of Portugal's Olivença claim but left the decision to Ferdinand VII of Spain, who declined to relinquish the one territory he stood to gain.[1]

If Portugal emerged from the congress minus part of what it

1. Damião Peres, in *Edição Monumental*, VI, 353–60.

desired, it must be remembered that small nations generally received slight consideration from the major European diplomats; Norway, for instance, was handed from Denmark to Sweden without consultation of Norwegian wishes. Had the legitimate Bragança dynasty, bound to Britain by alliance, not existed, Portugal might have found itself awarded to Spain regardless of its own feelings.

WAR'S AFTERMATH

Portuguese economy had been inevitably upset by the French invasions. Foreign trade had been all but ruined and the British had almost completely taken over the Brazilian market; even the nonindustrial United States had profited there from the paralysis of Portugal. Much of the home country had been fought over more than once in the recent wars. The French lived off the invaded soil, and the opposing British and Portuguese armies had often been forced to do the same. Peasants had been despoiled and often massacred by the invaders, and Wellington's scorched-earth policy in the Tôrres Vedras campaign had temporarily ruined the most productive part of the nation. After the French departure, the farmers returned to their homes and eventually repaired the damage, but so many returned penniless and half-starved that rehabilitation required longer than in other countries. The authorities tried to bring relief, but the ruin of trade and industry rendered them short of funds. The best they could do immediately was subsidize the manufacture of agricultural tools and take an economic census of the country.

GOVERNMENT FROM RIO

Prince John, despite his original reluctance to go to Rio de Janeiro, had grown to like his new home. Although he could safely have returned to Lisbon by 1812, physical indolence and his comfortable life in the tropics caused him to remain away for another nine years. In 1816, the long-overdue death of old Maria made him John VI (1816–1826), King of Portugal and Brazil. He had meanwhile taken important steps to favor and please his South American subjects which the Portuguese felt were in their own disfavor. He relieved Brazilian industries of heavy taxes, opened the ports of the country to world trade, established the Bank of Brazil to encourage commercial transactions, and went so far as to encourage science and permit the introduction of printing.

John took his greatest step in 1815, when he declared Brazil a kingdom equal in status to Portugal. For the seven years the connection between the two countries lasted, John ruled a "United Kingdom," a dual monarchy in which Brazil was no longer a colony but rather a partner. The two had approximately equal populations (about 4 million each), but the future could be foretold. Portugal was tiny; Brazil was vast and before many years the onetime colony would heavily outweigh the parent country.

John's relations with Carlota remained as bad as ever, and her disposition worsened until she found almost her only pleasure in intrigue. She sought to be named regent of Spain following her family's deposition by Napoleon, though how she expected to overcome the Bonapartist obstacle remains unclear. She also sought a throne for herself, as a Spanish *Infanta*, in the Río de la Plata, which had all but ended allegiance to her brother, Ferdinand VII, then a prisoner in France.

The princes, Pedro and Miguel, were growing up meagerly educated and neglected by their father. Pedro was by far the more intelligent, with some likeable qualities and a taste for music and verse; he later composed the Brazilian national anthem. Miguel was of impressive appearance, but wholly lacking in intellectual qualities, with interests that seemed limited to hunting, bullfighting, and fireworks. Contemporaries considered him only semiliterate at best. Neither could be considered a promising king for either Portugal or Brazil, but it seemed fortunate that Pedro was the older and likeliest to inherit. Under the right auspices, he might turn into a presentable monarch, whereas Miguel would be disastrous for any country.

THE CONSTITUTION AND THE BRAGANÇA RETURN

The man who came nearest to being an executive in Portugal was Marshal William Carr Beresford, who had retained his command of the Portuguese army. Competent as a soldier, he was heavy-handed and obtuse in politics and kept too many British officers in high Portuguese posts. The army became a center of discontent, partly because liberal ideas had penetrated and partly because of resentment at being dominated by foreigners.

Eventually, as had happened in the past, Portugal took its cue from Spain. That country had adopted a constitution in 1812 that was contemptuously suppressed by Ferdinand VII when he returned from French captivity. Ferdinand instituted a counterrevolutionary reign of terror in which he restored the Inquisition and seemed bent on returning his country to the times of Philip II. The liberal Spanish element endured this until 1820, when a military revolt compelled Ferdinand to swear allegiance to the Constitution of 1812. Beresford was in Rio at the time, and Portuguese army officers and masons felt this to be their opportunity. Revolts in Portugal grew too hot for the feeble Lisbon regency to handle and its members appealed to the man with greatest prestige in the country, Palmela. He advised them to call a côrtes, apparently extinct for some time in Portugal. The regency members felt reluctant to do this, but mutiny in the army and general violence compelled them to acquiesce and issue a call for a côrtes to meet on January 6, 1821. Beresford, returning from Rio, was refused permission to land at Lisbon and went to England and out of Portuguese history.

The côrtes, selected by a kind of popular election never known in its former days, assembled only a little behind schedule and prepared to give the nation a constitution. Its members, for the most part, were political novices and seemed to feel that Portugal's ills could be cured by oratory. There were many masons in the body, who insisted on using their ritual in acts of major solemnity.[2]

At long last, John VI decided to come home, having had it made clear to him that he must either return to his European kingdom or lose it. He left Pedro as his regent in Brazil, and a tradition avers that before departing, the king, aware that Brazil would soon secede, advised the prince to put himself at the head of any separatist movement in the expectation of becoming monarch of the new nation. When John, with the rest of his family, arrived on July 3, 1821, he was received with great celebrations but obviously felt uneasy about the whole situation. He had already accepted the côrtes and the (unseen) constitution in theory but was not prepared for such extremities as the recent exile of the Cardinal-Patriarch of Lisbon and the decreed exile and loss of Portuguese citizenship for all who would not swear allegiance to the constitution. In Brazil he had proved himself a statesman of some consequence, but he was physically

2. Fortunato de Almeida, *História de Portugal*, VI, 33.

timid and did not fit well into the new situation, having lost control of events in Portugal.

THE SEPARATION OF BRAZIL

The huge daughter country had been independent, except for the Bragança connection, since its elevation to the status of kingdom in 1815. The arrangement was now generally satisfactory to the Brazilians; their trade had grown, administration had improved, European merchants and scientists flocked there as never before, and intellectual life had quickened with the introduction of printing presses. There was another side to the picture—maintenance of the royal court at Rio was expensive; John's recent conquest of Uruguay had imposed a financial burden, and Brazilians resented the virtual monopoly by Portuguese of the higher political and military positions. Yet the gains far outweighed the inconveniences, and if the Crown could have stayed in Brazil the dual monarchy might have endured for years, because the House of Bragança remained reasonably popular.

When John returned home, many Brazilians feared Prince Pedro would soon follow his father. The Prince had to mollify such persons with the single word *fico* (I remain), uttered at the beginning of 1822. This was assurance that he had cast his lot definitely with Brazil, and meanwhile the côrtes in Lisbon gave every reason for anxiety. The majority of its members had no wish to treat Brazil as an equal but desired instead to regain control of it and make it a colony again. Brazil had been invited to send members to the côrtes but they found themselves in a hopeless minority, obliged to endure insults. In the streets of Lisbon they heard opprobrious remarks hurled at them to the accompaniment of hisses.

In Brazil, Pedro and his chief advisor, José Bonifacio de Andrade e Silva, the "Patriarch of Independence," were watching events carefully and steering Brazil toward independence. When the final declaration came, it had a rather stage-managed look. In June 1822, Pedro accepted the title "Perpetual Defender of Brazil." Two months later he issued a manifesto that fell just short of being a declaration of independence. He spoke the final word on September 7 when, as he travelled through the Province of São Paulo, a messenger from his wife, Leopoldina, overtook him with the latest dispatches from Lisbon. These made plain the determination of the côrtes to restore

Brazil to colonial status and furthermore decreed the arrest and trial of José Bonifacio. By the banks of the small River Piranga, Pedro turned to those with him and raised the cry "Independence or Death." He knew that he had behind him the powerful class of Brazilian planter-aristocrats and that Portugal absolutely lacked means to coerce him. Consequently, Brazil won independence almost bloodlessly, in contrast to neighboring Spanish America, where the bitter struggle in some places lasted fifteen years. Before the end of the year Pedro was crowned Emperor of Brazil in the Cathedral at Rio de Janeiro.

The new ruler, only twenty-four, had many problems to face, among them the gaining of recognition by foreign governments. The United States granted it first, in 1823, when President Monroe gave official audience to Pedro's envoy. Portugal attached small importance to this, for it was expected and did not break the solid European monarchical front. The Portuguese placed part of their hopes in the facts that Pedro was John's heir, that John would probably not live long, and that Pedro's accession to their throne would soon bring the two countries together again. They meanwhile proposed an impossible arrangement whereby John, with the title of emperor, should receive fealty from Pedro, who might otherwise govern Brazil as he pleased. But in 1825 the British showed themselves about to recognize Brazil, which, for commercial reasons, they could not wait much longer to do. George Canning, head of the Foreign Office, let Palmela, Portuguese Minister for Foreign Affairs, know that His Britannic Majesty's Government would shortly recognize Pedro and strongly recommended that His Most Faithful Majesty's Government preserve its dignity by doing so first. John VI, or those writing in his name, then "conceded" instead of recognizing Brazilian independence and followed with a considerable list of the rights and privileges he allowed his former subjects; rights which, needless to say, lay beyond his power to give or take. The British government soon recognized Brazilian independence and was followed by others.

MIGUEL AND THE CONSTITUTION

The new Portuguese constitution, which went into effect in 1822, declared all citizens legally equal and eligible to office, freed the press, removed class privileges, and placed most power in a single-house legislature over which the Crown had a suspensive veto. The Inquisition, already virtually dead in Portugal, had been formally abolished by the côrtes. John had accepted the constitution sight unseen before returning from Brazil, as had Pedro before severing his Portuguese connection. Carlota Joaquina and Miguel, both absolutists, refused to swear allegiance to the constitution and received sentences of banishment that were not carried out. John himself showed that he had rather a talent for being a constitutional monarch. "The best thing to do is to do nothing," he once said, and when reports from the côrtes were delivered to him he would say: "Well, let us see what they say I have done today." [3]

The energy, though not the brains of the Braganças in Portugal resided in Carlota and Miguel. Twice they organized insurrections designed to restore royal absolutism. The second, called A *Abrilada* because it took place in April 1824, was so dangerous that the king took refuge aboard a British ship in the Tagus, from which he supervised its suppression. Having found Miguel an unmitigated nuisance, he sent the prince on a tour of European courts, ostensibly to gain a much-needed education. John was then able to complete his life and reign, which lasted until early 1826, in comparative quiet.

The "king-emperor's" death confronted Portugal and Brazil with a problem both had foreseen. Pedro was heir by primogeniture, but had he forfeited his rights by seceding and becoming Brazilian emperor? He desired his father's throne, but the idea was intolerable to the Brazilians, who considered it only a disguised way of reannexing them to Portugal. Because Pedro had already lost much of his Brazilian popularity, he did not press the matter but worked out a compromise instead. He decided that Miguel, now twenty-four, should wed his daughter, seven-year-old Maria da Gloria, and that the pair should reign as joint sovereigns.

Miguel was now in Vienna, where he came under the influence of Metternich. The reactionary Austrian chancellor certainly disliked the Portuguese prince, but saw him as a promising agent for restoring in his country the absolutism Metternich desired for all Europe. Miguel seemed to accept Pedro's arrangement and while in Vienna went through a betrothal ceremony with little Maria, with the child represented by proxy.

He then returned in 1828 to Lisbon where Pedro had sent a

3. Marcus Cheke, *Carlota Joaquina*, p. 110.

Charter of Government to replace the 1822 constitution. He found the absolutists in the ascendancy and his own popularity high, and surrounded himself with the most conservative notables and priests. He went through some show of swearing allegiance to Pedro's Charter, but because a crowd of reactionaries surrounded him during the ceremony, few knew afterward exactly what oath he had taken. Everyone *did* know that he immediately began to behave as a *rei absoluto*. Pedro had sent his small child to Portugal, but those in charge of her learned before reaching Lisbon that the marriage arrangement had become a dead letter and took the girl to London instead.

For the moment, Miguel was supreme in mainland Portugal, but he had numerous Portuguese enemies elsewhere. Liberals began emigrating, many going to London where Palmela, now ambassador there, became a center of opposition to Miguel and informed the Duke of Wellington, then prime minister, that he recognized only the authority of Pedro. The Azores did not take kindly to Miguel and their governor soon pronounced in favor of Pedro and Maria. The English government never recognized Miguel, but Spain, Russia, France, the papacy, and the indifferent United States maintained diplomatic relations with him. Within the country, Miguel's chief supporters were the lesser nobles (the greater tending to favor Pedro because of his seniority), most of the churchmen, and probably the majority of the people. Those preferring Pedro were the business and professional classes, the conscientious liberals, and part of the army, including its ablest commanders.

From Brazil, Pedro worked in his daughter's behalf and sent what subsidies he could to Miguel's opponents. His brother, meanwhile, was giving Portugal a reign of small consequence. There was no blood bath of liberals, partly because too many were out of his reach; the main features were the restoration of the Jesuits and the founding of a new knightly order for the defense of Catholicism and the suppression of masonry. Miguel was injured in a carriage accident in 1828 and this had a sad effect on the nation, to a large part of which he was the "Angel-Prince." To the question of why Heaven could permit such a calamity to befall its favorite, some priests stressed the fact that his life had been spared, doubtless through the intervention of the Holy Virgin.[4]

The year 1830 proved important to Portugal for two reasons.

4. *Ibid.,* p. 195.

Dowager-Queen Carlota Joaquina died, and this removed a powerful bulwark of reaction. More important was the wave of revolution that swept through Europe, overthrowing the reactionary French government of Charles X and bringing the independence of Belgium, besides causing a Polish rising against the Czar. Brazil was not too far away to be affected, for there almost the last vestiges of Pedro's popularity disappeared and the emperor began to think of abdication.

Pedro did abdicate the next year in favor of his small son Pedro II, and sailed for Europe with but one idea in mind; to unseat Miguel and establish Maria da Gloria as Queen of Portugal. He had not been altogether liberal in Brazil, but now, from conviction or policy, identified himself completely with the Portuguese constitutionalists. He went first to England and then to France, where he managed to collect ships and gather the anti-Miguelist exiles. With these he went to the Azores, where his own supporters were in control. With what soldiers he could raise and the aid of Portugal's two best military leaders, João Carlos Saldanha and António José de Sousa, he sailed for the mainland in 1832 and seized Oporto by surprise. Miguel was momentarily taken off balance, but he soon besieged Pedro's small liberal army with a much larger one. This siege of Oporto lasted over a year, during which the Miguelists seemed several times on the verge of winning. In June 1833 Pedro tried a diversion and sent Sousa, now Duke of Terceira, in a fleet commanded by the English Charles Napier, to make a landing in the extreme south of Portugal. The move succeeded; Terceira approached Lisbon from the south and meanwhile Napier routed Miguel's squadron, thus giving Pedro command of the sea. Lisbon now lay open and Pedro left Oporto to enter the capital, where he sent the Papal nuncio, a strong partisan of Miguel, back to Rome.

The Miguelists raised the siege of Oporto but made some resistance for a time in the interior. Not until May 1834 did the younger brother finally yield to the elder by the Concession of Évora-Monte. Miguel received the right to remove all his personal belongings and collect a pension on condition that he leave Portugal forever.[5] Once in exile, he repudiated the agreement, saying that he had been compelled to sign it and did not consider it binding. Nevertheless, he never returned nor apparently attempted to do so. He died in Ger-

5. The terms of the concession are given in full by Peres in *Edição Monumental*, VII, 224–25.

many in 1866; his heirs continued to be pretenders and there were always some Miguelists in Portugal.

Maria, now fifteen years old, arrived in Lisbon in September 1834 and was at once enthroned with her father's charter as the basis of government. Pedro himself, though only thirty-six, was in the final stages of tuberculosis and had managed to live just long enough to see his daughter's cause triumphant. He died before the end of September and is known in Portuguese history as Pedro IV.

12

Two Decades of Confusion

NATIONAL PROBLEMS

With Miguel gone and the girl queen enthroned, Portugal profoundly hoped for decades of domestic tranquility, but the hope proved unfounded and the political situation remained explosive. Had Pedro lived he might have made a difference, but his death left inexperienced Maria, of Brazilian birth, which counted against her, a prey to contending factions. Liberals hated the Church, though the influence of the clergy upon the common people remained strong. The army unfortunately had grown accustomed to interfering in politics and, as the divine status of monarchy had unquestionably lessened, it was learning to make and unmake governments.

Portugal in the 1830s and 40s was an underdeveloped country by western European standards, which were coming to mean possession of railroads and mechanized industry. The liberals who created the first national constitution in 1822 were merchants and landed proprietors; there was no industrialist in the constituent côrtes.[1] Portugal as yet had no industry of the modern kind, and no apparent effort was made for decades to create one. Not until around 1842 did the country show signs of modernization. In that year it was

---

1. Joel Serrão, *Temas Oitocentistas para a História de Portugal no Século Passado*, I, 91.

estimated that Portugal had a total of twelve steam machines, half of them in Lisbon. At the same time, Belgium, with a smaller area, had 1,300. The Portuguese total had risen in the next decade to fifty-three with a total of 777 horsepower, still a pitifully small number.[2] There was as yet no railroad mileage, and in 1846 a speaker in the House of Peers stated that such lines were not yet practical for Portugal because the volume of traffic between Lisbon and Oporto, the busiest travel route, would not support them. He estimated that freight and passenger transit would need to multiply many times before a railroad could be anything but a loss.[3]

At the start of Maria's reign, progress in restoring the damages of the Peninsular Wars had been annulled by the ferocity of the Miguelist civil war. There was poverty in the land and the national debt stood high. Even after the secession of Brazil, Portugal possessed a colonial empire, mostly in Africa, and this lay stagnant and neglected. When Brazil seceded, some leading men in Angola thought seriously of abandoning Portugal and joining Pedro's new empire. John VI's governor showed energy in suppressing this movement, but Portugal took it seriously enough to insist in the recognition treaty that Pedro pledge not to attempt any such annexation.

MARIA DA GLORIA

Maria II (1834–1853) married a prince of Leuchtenberg early in 1835, but this first consort died of angina within three months. Early in 1836 she took Prince Ferdinand of Saxe-Coburg-Gotha (1816–1885) as a second husband, and they produced eleven children, two of whom became kings of Portugal. The queen's many difficulties must have been increased by the fact that she was pregnant during half her reign. Ferdinand became king by courtesy and was named commander-in-chief of the army, but tactfully never exercised the second function to any great extent.

At the outset of the reign, numerous *guerrilhas* committed depredations in the provinces and, though they claimed to uphold some political cause, they were, in effect, bandits. They robbed and terrorized citizens, and the official gazette, *Diário do Govêrno*, pretended, in the face of the government's obvious impotence, that they were

2. *Ibid.*, p. 120.
3. *Ibid.*, pp. 122–23.

performing public services in the interest of law and order. Portugal had no regular police force in most districts, and the magistrates with the duty of punishing the marauders were often of the same stripe.[4]

Maria's first prime ministers were Palmela, now a duke, Saldanha, and Terceira, all three of whom belonged to the liberal faction that had supported Pedro in his overthrow of Miguel. The Carlist civil war was now going on in Spain, with the followers of Don Carlos determined to overthrow the child queen, Isabel II, and restore the reactionary Spain of the past. Portugal was interested, for if Carlos won, as he seemed close to doing, there would surely be a powerful Miguelist revival at home. The Spanish war finally ended with the exile of Carlos in 1839, but meanwhile Spain influenced Portuguese affairs. In 1836 a group of Spanish sergeants had browbeaten the regent queen-mother into restoring the Constitution of 1812. This *coup d'état*, called the Revolution of La Granja, encouraged Portuguese radicals to demand restoration of their own 1822 constitution. They gained their objective by a combination of force and bluff, which brought to the fore a new man, Manuel da Silva Passos, commonly known as Passos Manuel. Because the constitution now restored no longer quite applied to the current situation, two years (until 1838) were consumed in bringing it up to date.

The public treasury had meanwhile grown so empty that the royal household lacked the means to pay living expenses. On the eve of her marriage to Ferdinand, Maria sadly wrote Palmela:

> I spoke to the Viscount of Pôrto Covo to see if he would give any money: he told me that he had not enough money in cash to give. This morning I also spoke to the Count of Farrobo telling him that we needed money, if he would care to give any on entering the Ministry of Finance: he refused in such a way that with such people there is nothing to do but beg God's patience to endure them.[5]

Evidently Palmela found means to assuage the royal wants, for court life continued, though not on the scale of John V or José. Not only the cash but the credit of the Portuguese state had disappeared, a condition a revamped constitution of 1822 would not remedy.

Passos Manuel's new ministry for constitutional restoration was called the Septembrist government because it came into office in

4. Fortunato de Almeida, *História de Portugal*, VI, 260.
5. Damião Peres, in *Edição Monumental*, VII, 249–50.

September 1836. There being no constitution in effect at the time, it ruled for two years by dictatorial decree. Passos took the ministerial post of *Reino* (Interior) and became the strong man of the administration. He proved to be a better orator than economist, once exclaiming theatrically: "What was my mission? What was the purpose of the revolution? What is it the people wanted on the 10th of September?" Answering his own questions, he said that they wanted: "the dogma of national sovereignty; they wanted a constitution given by the nation and not imposed by the Crown." [6]

It is doubtful that most of the people really cared greatly about the things Passos insisted they desired. What they truly wanted was a balanced budget, stable money, and the opportunity to live and work in peace.

For all Passos' perfervid oratory about national sovereignty, the Septembrists showed greatest interest in perpetuating themselves in office. One means was the reorganization of the national guard, a bulwark of the constitution, and the strengthening of its discipline. Another was the dismissal of many functionaries and bureaucrats who could not be counted on for political support, many of whom were removed merely to make places for deserving Septembrists. A contemporary wrote:

> Passos Manuel declared in the parliament that he had a tired arm from signing dismissals, and right there was one of the capital errors of the revolutionists. Instead of winning to the revolution all kinds of men, who because of their knowledge or preponderance could give it force, what they wished to do was avail themselves of offices to reward the services of their own people. And what people! Holy God! [7]

The September Revolution, instead of easing the national situation, made it worse. Some believed the royal family in danger; Leopold I of Belgium, uncle of Maria's consort, considered sending a relief expedition to Portugal, Palmerston reinforced a British fleet in the Tagus, and Louis Philippe dispatched several French warships to observe the situation. The queen herself left the Necessidades palace for suburban Belem, which was quieter than Lisbon.

The tension somewhat eased when members of the côrtes, weary

6. *Ibid.*, p. 253.
7. Almeida, *História de Portugal*, VI, 264.

of Passos Manuel, put embarrassing questions to him publicly. He and the entire ministry resigned; he never returned to power, though as a masonic grand master he continued to be influential in the country. The succeeding ministry was also called Septembrist, but the sterility of the entire so-called program had become apparent. Viscount Sá da Bandeira, though junior to the main leaders in the fight against Miguel, was now coming into greater prominence. He too was somewhat affiliated with the Septembrists, but, though liberal, was moderate compared to Passos Manuel and also probably the ablest statesman in the country now that Palmela was aging. When the two veteran marshals, Terceira and Saldanha, broke into military revolt in favor of Pedro's Charter, Sá da Bandeira forced them out of the country and reincorporated their forces into the national army.

The Septembrists next split, with Sá leading the moderate faction. He presided over the adoption of a modified Constitution of 1822, but his ministry proved short; the Charter had become popular again and even Passos Manuel, no longer in office, pronounced in favor of it. Another rising politician, António da Costa Cabral, became a vehement Chartist, and although the 1822 constitution remained in effect until 1842, Costa, with the help of Terceira, who had meanwhile returned, was then able to engineer readoption of the Charter. Palmela held the prime ministership for three days pending the formation of a Chartist cabinet. Terceira headed the new ministry, but Costa was its real leader from 1842 to 1846. By the revived Charter, Portugal acquired a bicameral legislature, the lower house elective and the upper a Chamber of Peers. One of Costa's first acts was to create enough new titles to give him a majority in the Peers, which was one reason his ministry lasted an unprecedented four years.

Public debt was the most pressing Portuguese problem, and all efforts by Costa Cabral and presumably Terceira also, failed to reduce it. The debt climbed until, in 1853, it reached the figure, in United States monetary terms, of $10 million—an amount trivial for Great Britain or France, but for Portugal, with its small national income and population, a distressing figure, especially because the normal revenues from taxes, customs duties, and stamps failed to balance the annual budgets.

Government was costly, and the financial efforts of this Chartist ministry, however sincere, went for nothing. Costa and his associates fostered the planting of groves of trees in empty, barren regions incapable of producing anything else. They encouraged scientific breeding of better cattle and empowered the existing Viniculture Company of the Alto Douro to administer a fund for the establishment of huge common winecellars advantageous in marketing the product. On its credit side, also, the ministry maintained law and order, although this required some press-gagging and management of elections. Portugal's standard of living seemed somewhat on the rise, but budgets remained unbalanced.

MARIA DA FONTE

Portugal experienced in 1846 an outbreak perhaps unique in nineteenth-century occidental society; the so-called rebellion of Maria da Fonte. Maria herself seems to have been a woman of the tiny hamlet of Fonte, distinguished for courage, though some believe her to have been a mythical heroine. The movement was called by her name because of the preponderant part women played in it. It stemmed from a government order which, for sanitary purposes, forbade further burials in church grounds and established public cemeteries away from towns and villages. To peasants, many priests, and especially women, this meant condemnation of the dead to eternal damnation. The outbreak apparently started at Tôrres Novas, in the Ribatejo province north of Lisbon, from which it spread rapidly. Detachments of troops sent to quell this rising were often repulsed by the infuriated peasants and their women, or, if they captured villages, they could not control the surrounding country.

As the rebellion spread, more sophisticated elements joined it; Septembrists, Miguelists, and some who merely hated Costa Cabral and the brother closely associated with him in government. Organized soldiers went over to the insurgents; a revolutionary junta was set up at Coimbra; southern Portugal began to witness risings; and the rebels swept nearly to Lisbon itself. The queen, realizing that the Cabral brothers were finished, named a ministry headed by Palmela, which included both Terceira and Saldanha, and which was soon joined by Sá da Bandeira. Costa Cabral took refuge in the Spanish legation, from which, with his brother José da Silva Cabral, he sailed to Cadiz.

The Palmela ministry, though in private agreement with Costa regarding the burial matter, had been selected to tranquilize the country and decided that the sooner the cemetery law became a dead issue the better. It seemed for the moment about to bring political peace.

THE CHURCH AND FOREIGN AFFAIRS

One of the last acts of the late Pedro's life had been to decree all religious orders abolished in Portugal. Their houses and lands were declared confiscated, although the government promised pensions to the members until they could be self-supporting. At the time of the suppression of the orders, tithing was also abolished, which made the financial situation of the Church difficult. This inevitably caused relations with Rome to deteriorate, one result being that when Portuguese bishops died no replacements were made and a growing number of sees stood vacant. The situation required a concordat with the papacy, but none was signed until the following reign.

Portugal found its most important foreign relations, those with Great Britain, revolving around African slavery and the slave trade. At Vienna in 1815, the Portuguese had agreed that their subjects should neither purchase slaves nor deal in them north of the equator. If the treaty was not well kept it was because Portugal's means of enforcing it were small. The British, who had abolished slavery in their empire in 1833, continued to press for compliance and Sá da Bandeira, a member of Maria's cabinet in 1836, at least made a sincere effort. He was the foremost abolitionist in Portugal, and he sponsored a decree in that year forbidding exportation of slaves by water or land from any Portuguese territory. This passed, but to the disappointment of Sá and many others, it proved unavailing. The governors of both Angola and Mozambique found that they could not enforce the law, and the latter merely handed in his resignation.

During the Maria da Fonte outbreak of 1846–1847, a brief foreign intervention occurred in Portugal. The revolt seemed to place the queen's throne and perhaps her life in danger, whereupon Great Britain, Spain, and France decided to assist her. This was partly arranged by Costa Cabral, who had meanwhile become Portuguese Minister in Madrid. It had the backing of Saldanha, the new leader of the government, who saw no other way of coping with the movement, now headed by a junta in Oporto. A Spanish army invaded Portugal through the Trás-os-Montes and a British fleet took some action against the rebels, though principally striving to stop the fighting. Peace came in 1847, when representatives of Great Britain, Spain,

Queen Maria, and the insurgent junta signed the Convention of Gramido. By its principal terms, the junta dissolved itself and a general amnesty was proclaimed.[8]

THE END OF MARIA II

The briefly interrupted civil strife soon reopened and continued as sterile as ever. The Constitution of 1822 and the Charter had become fetishes to be fought over by political leaders, mostly to cloak their own ambitions, and it is hard to see how one or the other could have made much difference. Palmela died in 1850, and this seemed to remove the principal element of stability left in Portuguese politics. But better times were at last in store. Saldanha seized power in 1851 and realized that for the time being Portugal had had enough of violence. He changed the name of his party from Chartist to Regenerator, and the Septembrists began to call themselves the Historic Party, though they gradually superseded this by the name Progressive.

Maria II, who had seen little peace in her lifetime, could at last enjoy some tranquility, but her remaining days were few. In nineteen years she had changed from a rather pretty girl to an overblown matron worn out with childbearing. Her eleventh confinement proved more than she could survive, and she died on November 15, 1853, aged thirty-four, while delivering a stillborn Portuguese prince.

8. Full text by Joaquim Carvalho, in *Edição Monumental*, VII, 325–26.

13

Steps of Progress

Pedro de Alcântara (1853–1861), eldest child of Ferdinand and Maria, was sixteen when his mother's death brought him to the throne. There was no discernible brilliance in his ancestry, yet some unaccountable accident of heredity made him the most promising prince and king in Europe. At the age of nine he was reading and understanding difficult Latin works. At twelve he was translating Cicero, Sallust, Livy, and Vergil and writing Latin letters to his tutor. He had an interest in all the arts and sciences and learned modern languages, with emphasis on French and English.[1]

Portugal had abandoned the old law by which a king could rule at age fourteen, so Pedro waited two years while his father acted as regent. He spent some of the intervening time visiting England, Belgium, Holland, Germany, France, Italy, and Switzerland, not as a mere tourist but as an observer and student, as the lengthy diaries he kept show. When the time came for him to rule in person, he was in every sense prepared. To a minister who had presented him with a resolution he had delayed in approving, he wrote the following

---

1. Ruben Andresen Leitão, *Cartas de D. Pedro V aos seus Contemporâneos*, has published a collection of the king's letters from January 1855 to September 1861, a few weeks before his death. Leitão also furnishes a biography, *D. Pedro V—um Homem e um Rei*.

day: "As I do not want to reproach myself for signing a paper I have not read, I kept it until this morning, and only today did I find time to read it." [2]

His short reign was unfortunate in that two severe epidemics took a heavy toll of life. Cholera appeared in the country in 1853 and, after briefly subsiding, broke out again in 1855 and 1856. The number of Portuguese deaths is unknown, but a reliable estimate for the capital reported over 3,000 fatalities. Yellow fever raged in Lisbon the year after the cholera and about 5,000 died of it there. Instead of fleeing the plague as most of his forebears would have done, Pedro remained at his post and visited the hospitals constantly, with a total unconcern for his own life.

On the political side, Pedro created the *caixa verde* (green box) in which complaints against the ministers or himself could be deposited and were sure to be read and considered. He refused to sanction a proposal by Saldanha, whose Regenerators were still in office, to fill the upper chamber with additional peers in order to carry a proposed law. This royal negative caused the downfall of the government, which was replaced by the Historicals headed by the Marquis, later Duke, of Loulé and Sá da Bandeira. Loulé was apparently a genuine liberal, or Progressive, as his party now began to call itself, but bad luck soon overtook him from the foreign quarter. A French ship named *Charles et Georges*, obviously a slaver, was taken by Portuguese authorities off Mozambique in 1857. There were over a hundred Negroes on board, and the authorities accepted their statement of the character of the vessel instead of the commander's, who said they were voluntary workers being transported to French Réunion Island near Madagascar. The news reached Lisbon, where Emperor Napoleon III's minister lodged a protest. The French monarch, posing for home consumption and striving to resemble his famous uncle, backed his envoy to the limit and sent a squadron to anchor by Lisbon. Portugal appealed to its British ally for help, but, because England felt indisposed to interfere, Loulé yielded to superior force and handed over *Charles et Georges*, which had been brought to Lisbon. France then demanded an indemnity, and King Willem III of the Netherlands was named arbiter to determine the amount. His verdict was that Portugal owed France 349,045 francs, which it paid with bitterness. The situation was absurd; Europe had agreed to stop the

2. Leitão, *Cartas de D. Pedro V*, p. 106.

slave traffic, yet the French emperor's precious "honor" had caused him to browbeat a weak nation genuinely trying to aid the humanitarian program.

The Progressives, with Sá da Bandeira as prime mover and the enthusiastic cooperation of the young king, almost immediately took an important step regarding slavery. The decree of 1858 stated that in exactly twenty years all slaves in Portuguese territories should be freed. The delay would give African slaveholders, some of them mulattos, time to prepare for the economic blow. By the expiration of two decades, Pedro V was long dead and his brother Luís reigned, but the decree was then enforced as planned. At least it was enforced in Angola; much of Mozambique was not under genuine Portuguese control and its native inhabitants practiced slavery themselves and cooperated with Arab slave traders.

Pedro was betrothed in 1857 to Princess Stephanie of Hohenzollern, who belonged to the Catholic branch of her family. A year elapsed and in 1858 the princess arrived in Lisbon and was married to the king. Tragedy immediately ensued, for within two months the young queen died of diphtheria. Pedro, who had known his bride just long enough to fall in love with her, mourned deeply, and during the remainder of his own short life appears not to have considered remarriage.

Political troubles continued on the domestic scene. The Loulé ministry fell from power in 1859, a few months after the close of the *Charles et Georges* incident and partly as a result of it. The venerable Duke of Terceira now made his final appearance at the head of a new cabinet that was Regenerator but staffed almost entirely by *novos* (newcomers) determined to bring about sweeping changes by the enactment of a vast reform plan. This created a deadlock in the House of Deputies, which was straightway dissolved, and the ensuing elections returned Terceira with a majority. When the new côrtes assembled in January 1860, its first task was the adoption of a concordat with the Pope regarding the *Padroado*. The word literally means patronage and in this instance it referred to Portuguese temporal authority over the Catholic Church in the Orient. The nation neither then possessed nor had ever possessed large territories there but it was the oldest Catholic power in that part of the world and remained the only solidly Catholic state represented on the Asiatic mainland. The Portuguese Padroado had existed in the past but had lapsed because of recent quarrels with Rome. This new concordat, to which Pius IX assented, restored the old rights of Portugal over every diocese in the East and missionary authority everywhere except for a portion of China. The arrangement was accepted by Portugal on February 6, 1860, and soon afterward Terceira died.

The next major event was the death of the king. Pedro V, for all his great ability, had never been physically robust. On September 29, 1861 he went with two of his brothers on a brief hunting trip to Vila Viçosa in the interior. They returned early in October, all very sick young men. Prince Fernando died first; the king followed on November 11. The other prince, Augusto, recovered and lived nearly thirty years. There was at first some doubt about the cause of Pedro's death, but an autopsy revealed that it had been typhoid fever. He was twenty-four and would probably not have lived long in any event because he suffered from a severe nervous disease. His disposition had been a melancholy one, and he used to say of himself, "My good mother said to me often when I was small 'your passion is for tormenting yourself.' She was almost right." [3]

By a coincidence, Pedro's two other brothers, Luís and João, who had been travelling in Europe at the time, returned at once to Lisbon, where João fell ill and died before the end of the year. Luís, born in 1838 and now twenty-three, took the throne while in mourning for three brothers.

Luís

Luís Filipe (1861–1889), King of Portugal and the Algarve, Duke of Oporto, and Duke of Saxe-Coburg-Gotha, reigned for nearly twenty-eight years, but his imprint on public affairs never equalled that of his brother, who effectively reigned for only six. He was a man of good common sense whose principal interests were music, sailing, and literature. He knew how to be a constitutional monarch and followed the course of his great grandfather, John VI, who had extolled the wisdom of doing nothing. He could play the cello, handle a boat, and translate Shakespeare, which he did with *Hamlet*, *The Merchant of Venice*, *Richard III*, and *Othello*.

The Portuguese Bragança family, so large at the late queen's recent death, had been suddenly reduced to two males. The king's

3. Damião Peres, in *Edição Monumental*, VII, 357.

father, Ferdinand, remained in health and vigor, but he was not of royal blood and though he ultimately married again, it was to his mistress, a German or Austrian singer named Elisa Hensler. For the preservation of royalty in Portugal, therefore, the most urgent need was to make Luís a husband and father as soon as possible. The bride found was Maria Pia, daughter of King Victor Emmanuel of Piedmont-Sardinia who, thanks to Camillo Cavour and Giuseppe Garibaldi, had just become King of Italy. The marriage was celebrated first at Turin, still the Italian capital, on September 27, 1862, with Loulé standing as Luís' proxy. Maria then came to Lisbon and again married the king, in person this time. Their eldest son, Carlos, the next and penultimate King of Portugal, was born less than a year after the marriage.

Luís abstained from political life as much as possible, but Portuguese politics were never more vigorously practiced than during his reign. The pattern that would prevail for the next half century, until the termination of the monarchy, had already become established. The two parties, Regenerators and Progressives, were both monarchist; Republicans had not yet appeared, although they would soon do so. Of the two, the Regenerators may be called the conservatives and the Progressives the liberals, though in many respects no great differences existed and even these tended to disappear as the years passed. They developed the system called *Rotativism*, which meant that they alternated in office. When it seemed time for a change or the public seemed tired of either, they rotated and the "ins" became the "outs," or, to put it more tactfully, the loyal opposition. There were local bosses called *caciques*, from an old Indian word brought by the Spaniards from the Antilles, whose business it was to deliver votes by one means or another at election times.

In one respect the two parties showed a difference. The European scramble for African territory was soon to begin, and the Regenerators pushed the Portuguese claims and explorations hardest, being determined that their country should gain its share. Most forward steps of note were taken when the Regenerators held office.

There appears to have been no great statesman in Portugal between 1860 and 1910, except possibly Sá da Bandeira, who died at eighty in 1876, but there were politicians above average, such as João de Andrade Corvo, Manuel Pinheiro Chagas, Henrique de Barros Gomes, and João Franco. There were wily politicians, too, of whom perhaps the wiliest was José Luciano Castro (1834–1914), a weak orator and a cripple in later life but most adroit in controlling the Deputies and manipulating votes.

ECONOMIC STEPS

An unbalanced budget and a staggering public debt both seemed endemic in Portugal. The debt had again risen during Pedro's reign, and by the death of Luís in 1889 it amounted to nearly $100 per person in the nation. Partly counterbalancing this was the fact that several decades without armed strife had permitted the standard of living and the total wealth of the country to rise somewhat, so that Portugal's general situation had improved. Nonetheless, the debt continued to plague both monarchistic governments and republican ones to follow. When banknotes began to depreciate, as they presently did, inflation set in and the bad financial situation grew worse.

At this time, all paper money was issued by the Bank of Portugal, dating from 1846 and formed by the amalgamation of two earlier banks. Shares were held by the government and the public; the governor of the bank was an official appointee and was considered a public servant. The Bank of Portugal's major problems came from the fiscal difficulties of the government, whose incessant demands for loans could scarcely be refused. A ceiling had been placed on the value of the notes the bank could issue, but this was raised from time to time; too frequently for the maintenance of sound currency.

There was a brighter side to the picture, however. A Regenerator Minister of Public Works, António Maria Fontes, on taking office in 1851, found that the country had only 218 kilometers of macadamized roads, no telegraph lines, and, of course, no railroads. A little over four years later he could report 36 kilometers of rails in operation out of Lisbon and two additional lines, to Vendas Novas and Sintra, being prepared. Fontes' picture of road construction was even brighter, with 92 additional leagues built and 24 more under construction. An electric telegraph, he reported, was in the course of preparation. Not all the program could be completed during the remaining time he held office, which was brief. A minister of the Progressive Party, Emídio Navarro, in power during the late 1880s, finished part of what Fontes had begun.

Agriculture continued to be the most important national occupation, and societies were formed, with government approval, to increase productivity. "Born Members" of such societies were those already engaged in farming, as well as local administrative officials, doctors of medicine, and magistrates. Associate and Corresponding Members consisted of all persons the Born Members felt could be of use in their deliberations and labors. Agricultural fairs and expositions, in which Portuguese products were exhibited, took place in all parts of the country.

Wine remained the principal product of the nation, but its volume of output received a setback in 1872 when the Douro vineyards were attacked by phylloxera—insects particularly deadly to vines. It required years to stamp out the blight, and meanwhile there was some thought of substituting tobacco for grapes in the Douro. This finally proved unnecessary with the discovery that a new type of vine would yield the same juice and yet resist the insects. Ultimately the region produced more wine than could be consumed domestically or sold abroad; a situation somewhat alleviated when Germany signed a treaty giving favored treatment to the Portuguese product.

Portugal began to mechanize industry in a limited way in the reigns of Pedro and Luís, most of it operated by steam. One reason for the slowness was the country's own high tariff policy and the fact that it did not itself produce the machines, which had to be imported at heavy cost. A submarine cable connecting Lisbon with Rio de Janeiro caused rejoicing in both Portugal and Brazil, because each country had long lost any resentment over the manner of political separation in 1822. Portuguese steamships connected the capital with the Madeiras, Azores, and parts of western Africa. Home communications continued to improve, and a British survey at the beginning of 1884 showed that there were then 1,245 miles of railroad, either opened or about to be opened, 2,900 miles of telegraph line, and 50 miles of municipal streetcar service. This certainly did not place Portugal in the van of progress, but it had considerably changed the country in the past three decades.

POLITICS AGAIN

Ecclesiastical affairs sometimes had a political tinge. Pope Pius IX summoned an ecumenical council to Rome late in 1869 to promulgate the doctrine of papal infallibility. Portugal could not be fully represented because a number of its bishoprics happened to be vacant. The Archbishop of Braga and four bishops asked to be excused from attending because of their age and bad health. Only four others finally went to Rome, accompanied by lesser clerics who could not vote. When the question of infallibility came to a showdown, either three or all four of the Portuguese bishops signed a petition protesting promulgation of the dogma because they believed the time inopportune, though they declared they would accept it if passed. The bishop of Funchal in Madeira went home before the council closed; the remaining three, evidently realizing that they had displeased the Pope, withdrew their objections.

Meanwhile, Spanish affairs once again threatened to involve Portugal. Queen Isabel II grew up and became unpopular, and a military revolt dethroned and exiled her in 1868. The army leaders, particularly General Juan Prim, continued to be monarchists and at once looked for a new ruler. Prim's choice of a king was Ferdinand, father of Pedro and Luís, who was still not old, and if this could not be arranged he was willing to accept Luís himself. The new Spanish succession question thus became involved with the old one of uniting the Iberian Peninsula under one ruler. Prim had a Pan-Iberian program which, regardless of who became king of a united Iberia, would mean the absorption of Portugal by its larger neighbor.

In the meantime, Marshal Saldanha, now approaching eighty, had returned to Lisbon from the legation he had recently occupied in Paris and, rallying army malcontents to his side, had engineered a *coup d'état* which brought him to power. He briefly held several of the portfolios in the new ministry himself. Saldanha had somehow been converted to Pan-Iberianism and used his new position of power to promote the candidacy of Ferdinand. The latter's acceptance of a Spanish throne would not of itself unite the two countries, but Luís would be his father's heir and in time would succeed him. The Portuguese people disliked the whole negotiation, which threatened to make them a mere appendage to Spain.

Ferdinand rather relished the prospect of being a king in his own right, but out of respect to his son and the Portuguese people would not accept the Spanish throne without guarantees that Portugal should remain independent. In the meantime Saldanha, largely because of the shrewd negotiations of Luís, had been persuaded to give up power in Portugal and accept the ministry to England in which post he served until his death six years later. The Spanish government refused to accept the terms Ferdinand imposed, so his prospects of a throne vanished. He retired from public life, married his singer friend, and died in 1885.

The Spanish crown was then offered to Leopold of Hohenzollern, and the violent objections of Napoleon III helped bring on the Franco-Prussian War. Prim next persuaded Amadeo of Savoy, a younger son of Victor Emmanuel of Italy, to be king, but the general was assassinated in 1870 just as the Italian prince reached Spain. Amadeo did his best to reign over a chaotic nation but gave up the attempt in 1873 and returned to Italy. The Spaniards then briefly tried a republic, but in 1874 recalled the son of exiled Isabel and enthroned him as Alfonso XII.

A Portuguese republican party made its appearance in a small way and elected a deputy from Oporto in 1878, though the movement had made little headway up to the time of Luís' death. Perhaps the most potent weapons of the antimonarchists were the political cartoons of the clever republican artist, Rafael Bordallo Pinheiro (1846–1905), whose unflattering portraits of Portuguese statesmen, especially in connection with foreign policy, certainly won recruits to his cause.[4]

Luís died in October 1889, at the age of fifty-one, and was succeeded by his elder son, Carlos, age twenty-six. Amid the sincere mourning for a rather popular king, no one suspected that Portugal stood on the eve of a foreign crisis that would cause national humiliation and threaten the end of the Bragança monarchy.

TWO LEADING INTELLECTUALS [5]

Alexandre Herculano de Carvalho e Araujo (1810–1877) was the foremost Portuguese historian of the nineteenth century. His fame as a writer of history has almost obliterated the fact that he was also a brilliant prose stylist and the author of novels and short stories, usually with some historical basis. While he was alive, his countrymen read more of his fiction than of his history, and much of the former continues to be published.

4. R. J. Hammond, *Portugal and Africa, 1815–1910*, p. 88.
5. The following section is based on Bell, *Portuguese Literature*; Harry Bernstein, "Alexandre Herculano: Portuguese Historian and Historical Novelist," *Journal of the American Portuguese Cultural Society*, II, 65–93; Hernani Cidade, "Alexandre Herculano," *Os Grandes Portugueses*, II, 285–94; Figueiredo, *Literatura Portuguesa*; and Clovis Ramalhete, *Eça de Queiróz*.

A romantic liberal in politics, Herculano found the Miguelist regime unendurable and, at the age of twenty-one, migrated to France and England. When Pedro of Brazil began the revolt against his reactionary brother, young Herculano hastened to join him and took part in the expedition from the Azores to Oporto and in the subsequent battles that led to Miguel's defeat and exile.

Herculano then took up writing in earnest, and at first concentrated on poetry, in which he was gifted enough to gain a modest reputation. He was already turning to prose when, in 1839, King-Consort Ferdinand obtained for him the post of librarian at the Royal Library at Ajuda. The salary was small, but it enabled Herculano to live and have access to the best books. He wrote of many subjects but meanwhile turned to the national past in earnest. It was the era of Buckle in England, Ranke in Germany, and Augustin Thierry in France, and Herculano, conscious of the backwardness of historical studies in Portugal, resolved to remedy the situation. In the years 1846–1853 he produced his *History of Portugal* in four volumes. It is by no means a complete history and proceeds only to 1279 and the end of the reign of Afonso III, but is nonetheless a scholarly landmark because in it Herculano brushed aside the pious legends that had been generally believed until then; one example being that of the miraculous appearance of Christ to Afonso Henriques at Ourique. In this and like matters, Herculano insisted on concentrating upon the genuine documents contemporary with the events and ignoring or spurning the later accretions.

The work had a poor reception in Portugal at first. It came under bitter attack from both the press and the pulpit, and Herculano was accused of impiety and lack of patriotism. Not only had he failed to demonstrate that Heaven had always had a special eye on Portugal but he had not shown one Portuguese as always a match in battle for any three foreigners. Herculano was, in point of fact, a strong nationalist with a deep respect for religion, but the attacks on his book by ignorant clergymen drove him into the anticlerical faction. He found the general reception of his outstanding work so discouraging that he decided not to continue after the fourth volume. Instead he took a species of revenge on the clergy by writing *The Origin and Establishment of the Inquisition in Portugal*, in three volumes, from 1854 to 1859. This has been considered biased and unfair by some, but Herculano was purposely striking back hard after the treatment he had received.

In 1867, Herculano resigned the post of Royal Librarian and retired to a country estate where he spent the rest of his life as a successful gentleman farmer. He found time to engage in literary debates, however, and opposed both the dogma of the Immaculate Conception and that of papal infallibility. By the time of his death, Portugal knew him to be its greatest intellectual and awarded him a public esteem he had not enjoyed in his active years.

Herculano was a romanticist; the outstanding realist of Portugal in the nineteenth century was José Maria Eça de Queirós (1843–1900). Born in a small community of northern Portugal, Eça, whose father was a man of means, studied law and took a degree at Coimbra. He showed small taste for legal practice, however, and after graduation became a young man about town in Lisbon, where he helped edit a literary journal. Later he had the experience of visiting Palestine and Egypt, where he witnessed the opening of the Suez Canal.

Eça spent much of his life outside Portugal, and this unquestionably affected his view of his own country. He served as Portuguese Consul at Havana, Newcastle-on-Tyne, Bristol, and Paris, where he died in 1900. In addition to these long residences abroad, he made brief visits to other countries. His works, therefore, display a cosmopolitan character. He wrote with facility, at times with exuberance, though the latter trait was modified in later years. He enjoyed great popularity in his own time, yet did not publish all he wrote; several of his novels were made available to the public years after he died.

Eça is best described as a realist with a liberal sprinkling of satire. His long stays abroad made him realize the backwardness of Portugal, which he attributed largely to the dominance of the clergy, a class he seldom lost the opportunity to castigate and lampoon. Another favorite theme was the superstitious ignorance of Portuguese women; as pronounced in the upper as in the lower classes. The two ideas were often combined, because the influence of the priesthood on the women was greater than on their husbands or sons. Another frequent topic was that of poverty combined with ill health, both abundant in Portugal. In the novel *Maias*, Eça describes a wealthy grandfather who approves his grandson's ambition to become a doctor by saying that nothing could be more proper in a nation whose favorite pastime is falling sick.

Besides *Maias*, the most famous novels of Eça are perhaps *The Crime (or Sin) of Father Amaro*, *The Relic*, and *The Illustrious House of Ramires*. Father Amaro is a youth whom circumstances have caused to enter the priesthood without the slightest vocation for it. Moreover, as the story progresses, one encounters few clergymen with any real vocation. Amaro seduces a young girl who dies in childbirth and he, rather contrite at first, is soon persuaded by his superior to forget the matter and become a smug, self-satisfied priest.

The Relic is inspired in part by Eça's youthful trip to Palestine and Egypt, and is the tale of a young Lisbon rake whose chief ambition is to keep a strait-laced, wealthy maiden aunt from knowing his real character because he hopes to inherit her fortune. In a frantic effort to escape her domination temporarily, and in the knowledge that she will never consent to finance a trip to Paris, he pleads for an opportunity to see the Holy Land. To this "Auntie" consents and young Raposo makes the journey, thoroughly enjoying himself in Alexandria with an English prostitute. He takes her nightgown as a souvenir when departing for Palestine, where he collects what *may* be a specimen from the original Crown-of-Thorns bush. With his two packages, he returns to Lisbon and there makes the fatal mistake of confusing the two and presenting the wrong one to his aunt. He is disinherited, the Church gets her money, and he is condemned to earn a living by hard work.

The Illustrious House of Ramires is the story of a young man, by no means a rake, descended from a line so noble and ancient that he is rather bowed down by ancestry. There is no very sharp plot; the book deals with his attempt to reconcile the noble family past with nineteenth-century realities.

Eça's remarks about Portuguese ill health applied well to himself, for he was never physically strong and died in middle life.

14

Africa

During the early nineteenth century, Portugal's holdings in mainland Africa consisted of a small Guinea territory and straggling settlements along the coasts of Angola and Mozambique. In the two latter cases, effective control did not extend far inland except for some authority up the Zambesi River from the east. Portugal nevertheless claimed that Angola had no eastern and Mozambique no western boundary; in short, that its jurisdiction extended through the African continent from the Atlantic to the Indian Ocean. The intervening territory had never been really explored, and before the European partition of Africa began the only man known to have crossed from ocean to ocean was the renowned Church-of-Scotland missionary, David Livingstone, who, in the 1850s had travelled from Luanda on the Atlantic to Quelimane near the mouth of the Zambesi. A few years later he discovered Lake Nyasa north of Mozambique, though he may possibly have had a Portuguese predecessor at some unknown date.

By 1875 European interest in Africa had so grown that Portugal realized it must take steps to safeguard its own claims. An expansionist, João de Andrade Corvo (1824–1890) then held the ministries of both Foreign Affairs and Colonies, and he persuaded the côrtes to vote 30 *contos*, or about $32,000, for a scientific expedition to inner

117

Africa that would make better known the Angolan hinterland. As leaders, he selected Major Alexandre da Rocha Serpa Pinto of the army and Lieutenant Commander Hermenegildo Brito Capelo and Lieutenant Roberto Ivens of the navy.

The three proceeded to Angola, where they fitted out an expedition. Inland, at Bié, for reasons never quite made clear, they had a difference of opinion, the two naval officers going their way and Serpa Pinto his. The likeliest explanation is that Brito Capelo and Ivens, who were modest men, intended to follow instructions for the exploration of inland Angola, while the flamboyant Serpa Pinto, impressed by Henry Morton Stanley's recent crossing of Africa from the east, wished to emulate his performance from the west. The navy men made a systematic exploration of Angola and emerged at the mouth of the Cuanza River in 1880.

Serpa Pinto, with his share of the equipment and a number of native bearers, went all the way across Africa to Pretoria and then to Durban, from which he returned to Portugal a year ahead of his erstwhile colleagues. They had done the real work but he had won the laurels, and his book, *How I Crossed Africa*, far surpassed in sales the one they wrote with a less pretentious title. Not everyone in Portugal accepted Serpa Pinto as a great explorer. Writing in *Comércio de Portugal*, July 16, 1879, a correspondent pointed out that the major had crossed Africa in record time with the obvious wish to reach civilization as soon as possible and that his so-called scientific and geographical observations had been hasty and utterly superficial.

In 1884, the three explorers went to Africa again with instructions from Manuel Pinheiro Chagas (1842–1895), Regenerator Minister of the Navy and Colonies. Serpa Pinto, with a naval colleague, Augusto Cardoso, was to proceed inland from Ibo, ascend the Rovuma River of Mozambique, and establish jurisdiction, through the local chiefs, over the Lake Nyasa region. Two hundred miles inland from Ibo, Serpa Pinto fell seriously ill and Cardoso had him conveyed to the coast and Zanzibar, where he eventually recovered. Cardoso, with a considerable Black escort, reached Lake Nyasa, where he found Church-of-England missionaries already in charge.

Brito Capelo and Ivens performed a long and arduous journey through Central Africa, from Mossâmedes on the Angola coast to Quelimane. They traversed about 4,000 miles, of which 1,500 were over country previously unseen by Europeans. Their provisions gave out and they lived on what game they could shoot. Theirs was by far the most important and difficult exploration by Portuguese in Africa and gave some substance to the claim of jurisdiction from sea to sea.[1]

THE POLITICAL AND DIPLOMATIC STAGE

Serpa Pinto became Portuguese consul in Zanzibar, where his hot-headed conduct nearly embroiled his country in war, and then went home to be elected a Regenerator deputy in the côrtes. His speeches in this body were always about Africa; for all his faults, he had become a man imbued with the patriotic mission of extending his country's possessions in Africa. Like most of his contemporaries, he had nothing but contempt for the African Black. On one occasion, July 22, 1887, addressing the chairman with the customary formality of the Chamber, he said:

Your Excellency may feel sure that the Black [Preto] is systematically wanting in the truth.

He never speaks the truth, especially to a white man.

Your Excellency, being a large [landed] proprietor, knows that this is also sometimes true of our villager. He is always on the defensive, and understands that the defensive means failing to speak the truth to the proprietor. . . .

One of the most difficult things in Africa is to get the truth out of the Blacks.

When we arrive, there is no one but the Portuguese, and, drinking a bottle of aguardente, they say: Viva Portugal!

When the English arrive, they say, drinking a bottle of cognac: God save the Queen!

And now, when the Germans arrive, they say, drinking a bottle of gin: Hoch der Kaiser!

No credence can be placed in the Black.[2]

Here he referred to the fact that Portuguese, Englishmen, and Germans had become rivals for influence with various kinglets and tribes-

1. Brito Capelo and Ivens described their extensive exploration in De Angola á Contra Costa, 2 v.
2. Diário da Cámara dos Senhores Deputados. Sessão de 22 de Julho de 1887, p. 1375.

men. The whites brought presents, often alcoholic, and their own flags, and the natives gladly accepted the gifts and hoisted the flags until the next European party arrived.

African affairs had already reached the partition stage, and in 1884, Bismarck, seconded by France, had invited a congress of powers to meet in Berlin late that year. Six Portuguese delegates took part: "They attended with the unenviable distinction of representing the weakest power present and of having no allies save England, who could not be counted on for much since it felt that the Portuguese should know their place and assume a poor-relation status." [3] They stoutly upheld their claims, however, and returned from the congress with a title to Cabinda and Massabi, an enclave ultimately bounded by the French Congo and the Congo Free State under the presidency of Leopold II of Belgium. They also made sure of a frontage at the mouth of the great Congo River which they still called Zaire.

The most important decision the Congress made was that possession of territories in Africa, hitherto considered *res nullius* (no one's affair) in international law, must be effective in order to have validity. This was, on the whole, sensible, and Portugal accepted it and the international treaty, though not without some protests at home.

Nothing had as yet happened to interfere with Portugal's claim to a corridor from Angola to Mozambique, but it seemed wise to secure international sanction for it at the earliest possible time. In a treaty with France, signed May 12, 1886, the French republic agreed that His Most Faithful Majesty of Portugal "should exercise his sovereign and civilizing influence in the territories which separate the Portuguese possessions of Angola and Moçambique." [4] At the end of the year a treaty with Germany, which arranged boundaries between Angola and German Southwest Africa and Mozambique and German East Africa, said much the same regarding the interior corridor. The Portuguese afterward seemed to think that these treaties furnished guarantees of their claims, whereas the French and Germans merely meant that they had no objections to them.

The principal difficulty finally lay with Great Britain, which proclaimed a protectorate over Bechuanaland in 1885, bringing its boundary up to the Zambesi. What for the moment interested the

3. Charles E. Nowell, "Portugal and the Partition of Africa," *Journal of Modern History*, XIX, 12.
    4. E. Hertslet, *The Map of Africa by Treaty*, II, 675.

British most was the Lake Nyasa region, where the Churches of England and Scotland both had missions and where British-owned steamers plied across the water. The problem was that Portugal also claimed the lake and seemed as much interested in it as in the corridor across the interior. Lord Salisbury, both Prime Minister and Foreign Minister of the United Kingdom, once said that he could risk the wrath of Portugal but never that of Scotland, which was rather more pious than England and the birthplace of David Livingstone. Salisbury sent an emissary to address a conclave of the Church of Scotland and to propose, in the interest of amity, that some Portuguese jurisdiction over Nyasa be allowed, with guarantees for Protestant missions. The Scots "sat with faces like granite," [5] whereupon His Lordship abandoned that line of policy.

FURTHER PORTUGUESE PENETRATION

The Lisbon government published a *Mapa Côr de Rosa* (Rose-colored map) that illustrated national claims to the interior of Africa. There were several editions, because plans for boundaries changed slightly. It caused the British, who were now uncertain that they meant to allow all this, some alarm. They also worried over the two Portuguese expeditions to the critical parts of Africa in 1888, one headed by the experienced Africa hand, Artillery Major Joaquim Paiva de Andrade (1846–1928), assisted by Lieutenant Vitor Córdon, and the other by António Maria Cardoso. The leaders had secret instructions, though clearly Paiva de Andrade was bound for the interior and Cardoso for Lake Nyasa. Because the British knew approximately what the Portuguese wanted, the latter were unnecessarily mysterious about the two expeditions.

Cardoso was bound for Lake Nyasa to establish jurisdiction over native kinglets there. He actually reached the lake with a well-armed force, but hardship and want of food forced him to return to Portuguese territory. Paiva de Andrade had orders to occupy a series of points between the Limpopo and Zambesi Rivers, as far west as possible, "in order to enable the government, when the time comes, to have a positive basis for revindication of Portuguese rights when it is a matter of establishing, by diplomatic means, the Portuguese and British limits of action." The order named several tributary rivers

5. Quoted by A. J. Hanna, *The Beginnings of Modern Nyasaland and North-Eastern Rhodesia, 1859–95*, p. 138.

on whose banks it would be advantageous for the Portuguese flag to fly, all well to the west.

Paiva de Andrade and Córdon at once proceeded to Mozambique, where they carried out some of the orders until circumstances compelled the abandonment of the plan. While Paiva remained mobile and traversed the country, making friends with interior chiefs, Córdon established a fortification on the banks of the Sanyati, and received the allegiance to Portugal of tribesmen there.

Knowing something of the Portuguese expeditions, Salisbury decided to compromise and instructed George Petre, British Minister at Lisbon, to propose to Foreign Minister Henrique de Barros Gomes of Portugal that in return for a free hand north of the Zambesi the Portuguese should abandon claims of jurisdiction over Lake Nyasa. When Petre made the offer on October 30, 1888, Barros Gomes flatly turned it down, saying that such a treaty would never pass the côrtes.[6] Behind Barros' refusal lay the expectation that the expeditions of Paiva and Cardoso would furnish Portugal a better bargaining position. Furthermore, because he had been educated in Germany and was pro-German, he fondly hoped that Bismarck's empire would give Portugal backing in what it wanted.

RHODES, JOHNSTON, AND CALAMITY

The greatest danger to Portuguese ambitions came from Cape Colony, where Cecil Rhodes had founded his Chartered Company, heavily capitalized, with which he meant to push as far northward as possible. Rhodes, on a trip to London in 1888, met Harry (later Sir Harry) Johnston, who had just been appointed Her Majesty's Consul at Mozambique, though he also had every intention of increasing British influence in the interior. Learning that the consular salary would be £800 a year, Rhodes said that such an amount would never do for the work Johnston was about to perform and wrote a check for £2,000, with the assurance that there would be plenty more when necessary. Johnston, reaching his post, did not tarry long at Mozambique and was soon on his travels in the region south of Lake Nyasa, where he made friends with native chieftains and, being well equipped with presents, won them to the British cause.

Toward the end of 1889, Portugal felt the time had come to

6. Marquês do Lavradio, *Portugal em África depois de 1851*, p. 255.

implement the "Rose-Colored Map" plan. Henrique Paiva Couceiro, an army officer, was ordered to march eastward from Angola into Barotzeland and peacefully turn the local king into a vassal of Portugal. The Governor General of Angola, on relaying the orders from Lisbon, said that an identical expedition would move westward from Mozambique, but that Paiva Couceiro's would be expected to arrive first. In the meantime, however, Harry Johnston had encountered Serpa Pinto and his considerable armed force along the Shire River flowing northward into Lake Nyasa. An argument arose between them, because Serpa had come to chastise the unruly Makololos, most of whom had been brought to the area by Livingstone a generation earlier, and Johnston declared them under the Queen's protection. The Makololos helped solve the question by attacking the Portuguese expedition and being severely defeated.

The news quickly reached London and Lisbon by cable, and Petre soon received from Salisbury the terms of a drastic ultimatum to present to the Portuguese authorities. Its conditions were severe: (1) withdrawal of all Portuguese military forces from the Shire and other areas in dispute; or (2) withdrawal of the British minister from Portugal in the event of failing to receive a satisfactory reply within twenty-four hours.[7]

This was a calamitous beginning for the reign of young King Carlos. The ultimatum had been presented on January 11, 1890, and his government had until the following day to give its answer. Instead of a cabinet meeting, the ruler summoned a Council of State, consisting of both active and retired political figures and various military men of prestige. Some of those present urged rejection of the British demands for the sake of national honor, confident that major European powers would support Portugal. Others pointed out that the British could easily seize all Portuguese colonies speedily and that they might never be recovered. Still others believed the question should be submitted to general European arbitration. The final decision to yield seems to have been mainly the king's, whereupon the council drafted a reply to Petre and Salisbury in which Portugal, under protest, submitted to the British terms.[8]

The ministry straightway resigned; Prime Minister Luciano de Castro was succeeded by António Serpa Pimentel. Ernesto Hintze-

7. Nowell, *Journal of Modern History*, XIX, 15.
8. Francisco José Rocha Martins, *D. Carlos. História de seu Reinado*, p. 184 ff.

Ribeiro took the Foreign Office and Cesar Barjona de Freitas was sent to London to make a treaty with England on a new basis, the Mapa-Côr-de-Rosa issue being obviously now a dead matter. Negotiation of this treaty required months, and the Portuguese côrtes rejected the first version presented to it. But because the British proved unyielding, the second treaty, presented and adopted in 1891, did not improve the Portuguese position in Africa. It established the boundaries of Angola and Mozambique substantially where they have been ever since.[9]

The surrender caused by the British ultimatum was extremely humiliating to Portugal. The public, the press, and some politicians denounced their own government. The House of Bragança, though hardly responsible for the disaster, received scathing criticism and lost much popularity. It became a common saying that the Anglo-Portuguese alliance had made the nation merely a vassal of England and that it existed primarily to keep the subservient Braganças enthroned. Republican propaganda, not hitherto prominent, became outspoken, and leading persons not previously affected by republicanism began to turn toward it as a new hope.

There were bitter debates in the côrtes between Barros Gomes, and figures like Pinheiro Chagas, who a few years earlier had thought themselves on the verge of realizing the Mapa-Côr-de-Rosa plan. To say that it had been doomed to failure from the start and to call it a dream is to be governed altogether by hindsight. Both France and Germany, and briefly England, had thought the plan a feasible one, and Portugal very nearly realized its ambition.

9. James Duffy, in his *Portuguese Africa*, surveys the entire Portuguese experience in Africa. R. J. Hammond, *Portugal and Africa, 1815–1910*, and Eric Axelson, *Portugal and the Scramble for Africa, 1875–1891*, devote themselves especially to Portugal's role in the partition, Hammond from the European and Axelson from the African point of view. Ronald H. Chilcote, in his *Portuguese Africa*, is primarily concerned with the situation after the ultimatum.

15

The Triumph of Republicanism

CARLOS

Carlos (1889–1908), whom Portuguese monarchists sometimes still hopefully call Carlos I, was physically unrepresentative of his country. Some of his ancestors had been German and Austrian, and the king, blond and teutonic appearing, looked more like a German Field Marshal than a King of Portugal. Even in youth he had a tendency to stoutness, which became more pronounced as he grew older. Carlos possessed considerable intelligence; he resembled his father in devotion to the arts and had some flair for science, especially marine biology. He had been married since 1886 to Amelia of Orleans, daughter of the French Pretender, and the royal couple had two sons, Luís Filipe and Manuel, of whom the second became Portugal's last king.

Carlos' reign began under sad circumstances, his popularity injured by unavoidable capitulation to the British ultimatum, and ended with his assassination less than nineteen years later. He ruled in an era of murder of heads of state, for a president of France, a Spanish premier, an Austrian empress, a king of Italy, a president of the United States, and a king and queen of Serbia preceded him to the grave as a result of assassins. When he died the time was not far distant when the most important murder of all, that of Franz Ferdinand at Sarajevo, would precipitate World War I.

125

SIGNS OF POLITICAL INSTABILITY

The first violent manifestation of republicanism occurred in 1891, when troops of the Oporto garrison mutinied. They marched to the Praça D. Pedro in the center of the city, entered the municipal building, and hoisted a republican flag. But the revolt had been hastily and badly organized and, once the city seemed to be in the soldiers' possession, a longwinded orator began to bore them; soon his audience was lost, and the troops wandered away. Because the municipal guard had not gone over to the revolution and had blocked the streets to the telegraph office, some of the soldiers began marching in that direction. The column was halted by a great crowd, apparently of well-wishers, who formed such a packed throng that a breakthrough by the troops became impossible. Soldiers and civilians mingled and the march lost all semblance of a military movement. The civic and army authorities, who first had been overawed, regained their courage and assembled units that had not joined the revolt. The mutinous troops, meanwhile, having lost their unity, seemed already to have had enough of republicanism, and, when some shooting occurred, did not even prove a match for the less-trained municipals. A remnant made a stand in the civic building but were soon routed. Within a few hours of the outbreak matters were normal again in Oporto, but the national government could not find much comfort in the situation. Had the movement been better organized, it could have spread to other cities and swept the monarchy away then and there.

GUNGUNHANA

The Vatuas were a branch of the warlike Zulus living in southern Mozambique, and their ruler for some years had been Gungunhana. He ruled a large warrior people and could put 20,000 men of excellent fighting stock in the field. He was a physical coward and probably a cannibal, but the obvious power he wielded had caused him to be courted by both the Portuguese and the British. Gungunhana had for a time permitted a Portuguese resident at his *kraal*, but the question of just how subservient he was to this authority has never been answered; he certainly behaved as he pleased and accepted presents from any quarter. A Britisher who knew this king called him a "great fat humbug," but there was nothing sham about his warriors, armed with *assegais* (spears) and in some cases rifles.

Late in 1894 Gungunhana chose to turn against the Portuguese, and the seaport of Lourenço Marques, at the extreme south of Mozambique, was invested and seemed on the verge of falling. The home government sent out a royal commissioner, António Enes, a noted political and journalistic figure and always a champion of a greater Portuguese empire. Enes was soon followed by troops from Europe, a phenomenon almost unheard of, because Portugal had customarily relied on Black recruits. Colonel Eduardo Galhardo commanded, and with him were such dashing officers as Paiva Couceiro and Joaquim Mouzinho de Albuquerque. Once Lourenço Marques had been made safe, the Portuguese began undertaking expeditions into the interior, where they defeated first the Vatua king's allies and finally Gungunhana himself at the Battle of Lake Coolela, on November 7, 1895. Galhardo won by forming a square and defending it with rifles, small artillery, and the primitive machine guns then existing. The magnificent Vatua warriors charged numerous times, only to be mowed down, until the Portuguese cavalry, headed by Mouzinho, put them to flight. Galhardo then immediately advanced and captured Manjacase, Gungunhana's principal town, while the king fled to Chaimite, in a more secluded area. Enes and Galhardo returned to Portugal soon after the battle, deeming the work substantially finished, but Mouzinho, who remained, determined to capture Gungunhana himself. He did so after a rapid, daring march with a very small escort; he entered Chaimite, arrested the ruler, and humiliated him by making him sit on the ground in the presence of his subjects. Mouzinho then shot those of Gungunhana's advisors who had urged hostilities against Portugal and took the monarch away as prisoner. The captured king was sent to Lisbon and then to the Azores, where he ended his days in 1906.

Mouzinho eventually became Governor of Mozambique and later tutor to the Portuguese heir apparent, Prince Luís Filipe. For reasons never explained, except that he had occasional fits of melancholia, he ended his life by suicide in 1902. During his last seven years he was a national hero, and his name is still remembered in Portugal.[1]

1. The Vatua war and other exploits by Mouzinho are covered in Eduardo de Noronha's *Mousinho de Albuquerque*. Highly relevant also is António Enes' *A Guerra de Africa em 1895*.

Domestic Troubles and Foreign Relations

The alternation of parties in office continued during the 1890s, but the people of Portugal were obviously losing confidence in both the Progressives and the Regenerators. The victories in Africa did something to bolster the sagging prestige of the throne, but the financial picture remained as dismal as ever. A Regenerator cabinet, headed by Ernesto Hintze-Ribeiro and João Franco governed the country from 1893 to 1897 and at first showed liberal tendencies, such as restoring various freedoms lost during a recent semi-dictatorship by the Progressives. But it then took a harsher stand regarding newspapers and public assemblies, because both proved generally hostile to the government. The House of Peers was partly elective, a factor that increased the ministry's troubles, and an amendment to the constitution abolished that part of the upper chamber. As a result, in the next elections for the House of Deputies, so many of the opposition ostentatiously refrained from voting that an all-Regenerator côrtes resulted. Although it was able to give a parliamentary look to its proceedings, anyone could see that the cabinet governed dictatorially. An apparent attempt made on the life of the king, arranged, as some thought, by *agents provocateurs*, led to the enactment of a severe decree by which those suspected of anarchistic ideas and practices should be tried by a secret court and exiled to Timor in the East Indies. The unpopularity caused by this decree forced the Regenerator ministry to resign in 1897. The Progressives, who had regained some strength in the Deputies, replaced it with a ministry headed by their veteran José Luciano de Castro.

Carlos, as protocol demanded, made the visits required of a new sovereign to the capitals and courts of Europe. He went first to France, in 1896, and found the authorities, who were embroiled in the uncomfortable Dreyfus affair, far from cordial. There was still considerable monarchist sentiment in Republican France, and Carlos happened to be married to the daughter of the Orleanist pretender to the throne. The presiding officers of both the Senate and the Chamber of Deputies made a point of ignoring an official banquet given in the king's honor, and other ways were found of making Carlos feel less than welcome.

Visits to monarchical Germany and England passed smoothly

enough, but a trip to Italy caused friction with the Pope, at that time Leo XIII. The Italian government and the papacy had been at odds since the seizure of Rome by Victor Emmanuel in 1870, and Carlos was the nephew of the reigning sovereign, Humbert I. Leo demanded, as a token of respect, that Portugal's king visit him at the Vatican before proceeding to the royal residence at the Quirinal. This placed Carlos in an awkward situation, but he decided that family considerations came first.

These touchy questions of prestige proved minor in comparison with the danger that soon threatened Portuguese Africa from Great Britain and Germany. Because of its unstable finances, Portugal fell in arrears of interest payments on English and German loans. The regime of Bismarck had long since ended, and Kaiser Wilhelm II, as well as most of his people, felt dissatisfied with the parts of Africa they had obtained during the recent partitions. "In the expectation that Portugal would approach one or the other of them, and desiring that she would not turn to France, the two countries agreed to reply that they could only finance her jointly, and that as security for a large loan the colonies should be pledged or ceded." [2] In a secret (for a brief time) treaty late in 1898, they divided most of overseas Portugal into spheres of interest. Southern Mozambique, northern Angola, the Azores, Madeira, and the Cape Verdes would go to the British, and Germany's share would be southern Angola and northern Mozambique. The English safeguarded the Portuguese alliance by providing that a partition would be carried out only if Portugal proved willing to sell.

The agreement came to nothing, because it had been based on the assumption that Portuguese finances would straightway collapse. They did not, and the following year the Boer War broke out, in which the British needed some collaboration with the authorities of Lourenço Marques. Accordingly, the Treaty of Windsor was signed in 1899 by which the British guaranteed full protection to Portugal in return for its refraining from declaring neutrality in the South African War. The death of Queen Victoria in 1901 and the accession of Edward VII somewhat improved Portugal's position, because the new king liked Carlos and did not wholly lack influence in British foreign policy.

2. G. P. Gooch, *History of Modern Europe, 1878–1919*, p. 302.

POLITICS AGAIN

The Progressive Ministry of Castro lasted until 1900, when the Regenerators of Hintze-Ribeiro took office again. João Franco, who had begun to surpass Hintze in importance, or at least in vigor, did not take a ministerial post this time. Instead, he began to utter criticisms of his own party in the côrtes and show signs of bolting. Regardless of whether the particular land question over which he raised an issue was very important in his mind, Franco soon ceased to be a Regenerator leader and seceded with twenty-five other deputies. Hintze then regarded him as a particular enemy, and until his own death in 1907 made every effort, unsuccessfully, to crush him.

To combat the seemingly growing importance of the Republicans, Hintze, by a kind of gerrymandering, rearranged the voting districts of the country so that the influence of cities, where antimonarchism was strongest, would be outweighed by that of the rural districts. The move proved temporarily successful and at the next general election in 1901 no Republican gained a seat in the deputies. Franco, though a monarchist himself, also lost his seat and for the moment was silenced. Hintze meanwhile sponsored decrees and plans for reducing both the foreign and the domestic debt, but these brought no visible improvement.

Franco did not accept his temporary defeat, and in 1903 organized the Regenerator-Liberal-Center Party and talked vehemently in favor of liberal reform, improvement of public education, and decentralized administration of the country. He condemned the practice of rotativism, whereupon the two older parties joined in their hostility to him. "*Franquismo*," as the new ideas came to be called, spread rapidly through the provinces, though republicanism spread equally fast.

Portugal had grown weary of rotativism, in which the Progressives were still represented by old Castro and the Regenerators by Hintze-Ribeiro. Its people had learned during many frustrating years that it made little difference who held office. The parties represented no fundamental differences as did the British Liberals and Conservatives, and were alternately merely the "ins" and the "outs." Republicanism, shallow and naive though it was in Portugal, continued to grow.

It is hard to estimate the popularity or unpopularity of King Carlos. He had considerable ability, and today, long after his death, Portuguese continue to write favorable biographies of him and call him much maligned. But he had undeniably expensive tastes, such as ownership of a royal yacht, and liked to meet the King of England and the Kaiser of Germany on social and convivial terms that the slender Portuguese resources scarcely permitted. One count against him, alleged then and proved after his death, was that his ministers secretly supplemented the royal revenue by giving him sums from the public treasury. The Portuguese Civil List, meaning the yearly amount provided the Braganças, had become insufficient owing to depreciations of the national currency.

Portuguese republicanism had such intellectual leaders as Teófilo Braga, professor of literature at Coimbra, and the poet Abilio Guerra Junqueiro. Politicians defected from monarchism to republicanism because they saw in it the rising cause. Portugal had only a small industrial proletariat, but many city inhabitants in those precommunist years came to believe republicanism a cure for all ills in much the way the next generation in other countries embraced Marxism. There finally emerged the *Carbonaria* Society, an organization formed to spread revolutionary propaganda in the armed forces and civil service, and in no way opposed to violence.

THE FRANCO DICTATORSHIP

After Hintze-Ribeiro, there was a Castro Progressive Ministry of short duration, following an election in which both Franco's followers and Republicans showed gains. Debates in the côrtes now at times became shouting contests, and in one case Republican José Maria de Alpoím so heckled a Minister of the Interior that the latter could not finish a speech and parliament recessed for the day. An election of February 1906 brought Hintze-Ribeiro back into office, and he found the political situation so grave that he proposed to the king the closing of the parliamentary session, meaning that he and the cabinet would rule with dictatorial powers. Carlos pondered the request and replied in writing:

My dear Hintze, . . . I thought all night about your request and delayed answering until now because I did not wish to give a reply without considering myself absolutely able, through some information I then lacked, to reply as my conscience tells me I ought to do.

You feel, with the government under your presidency, that you cannot proceed in the present situation unless I grant the closing of the côrtes which is due to continue meeting next month, and furthermore that I should do this by a simple decree without hearing previously [the opinions of] the Council of State. You added that with this done you will take the responsibility for reestablishing a normal state of affairs in Lisbon, which has not been interrupted in the provinces.

It does not appear convenient to me to close the côrtes, because this would lead to a revolt of public opinion; not only of the republicans —that would be natural—but also of all the monarchists who are not with you on the present occasion. This would be certain, and we should not have any illusions about it. All we would do would be to add to the number of malcontents . . . a mass of people who hitherto have not been discontented. . . . By doing this, the government would only be able to save itself by violence and terror, and evil will befall those who only know how to govern in such a manner. . . .

You, Hintze, and your colleagues think in one way and I in another, which, in all conscience, I believe to be the better.[3]

The letter was a plain invitation to resign, and Hintze immediately did so, after which no one remained but Franco to be called to power. The new prime minister was honest in an environment of corruption, was loyal to the monarchy, and possessed courage and resolution. Determined to save the kingship, he expected to do so by establishing an incorruptible government and cutting expenses. He began the second course by abolishing sinecure offices, by which he saved about $250,000 and created so many enemies that Regenerators and Progressives closed ranks against him. After two months they forced him to offer his resignation, which the king would not accept. His Majesty felt far more confidence in Franco than in Hintze-Ribeiro, and, seeing now no other way of carrying on the government, handed the former almost the powers he had denied the latter. For the rest of Carlos' life and reign, Franco ruled Portugal virtually as a dictator, though he denied creating a dictatorship and declared that he governed constitutionally.

Certainly Franco underestimated the strength Republicanism had now attained in Portugal. He spoke confidently of shipping leaders of the movement off to Africa and published a decree to that effect, reluctantly signed by the king on February 1, 1908, the very day of the royal assassination. But Franco shrank from proceeding to ex-

3. Rocha Martins, D. Carlos, pp. 483–84. This work contains the best account of the reign of Carlos.

tremes against known Republicans and evidently felt them to be less physically dangerous than was really the case. A few Republican deputies were forcibly expelled from the côrtes when they grew obstreperous, but were allowed back the following day. Long and heated debates prevented the vote on any decrees Franco proposed, until the houses of parliament were closed by the king's order. As a next step, the dictator empowered administrative authorities to suspend newspapers and other publications injurious to public order. In this troubled way, Portugal got through the year 1907.

THE ASSASSINATION

Late in January 1908, the royal family paid a short visit to Vila Viçosa and on February 1 they returned to Lisbon, travelling the last stage by steamer. The king, queen, and the two princes left the waterfront and entered an open landau carriage bound for the Necessidades Palace. Crowds thronged the streets and suddenly a shot was heard, followed by screams and great confusion. A young man had pushed through the spectators and fired a pistol at Carlos, who evidently died instantly. The coachman whipped the horses to a run to get the rest of the family to safety, but, as he rounded a turn, a bearded man took careful aim with a rifle at Prince Luís Filipe and dealt him a mortal wound. A second shot wounded Prince Manuel slightly in the arm. The carriage dashed to the marine arsenal, where there was a medical department. The king was found to be dead, and Luís Filipe expired within minutes.

Meanwhile, the police had used their sabers on the killers and almost literally chopped them to pieces. The youth was identified as Alfredo Costa, cashier of a Lisbon store, and the bearded man as Manuel Buiça, a village schoolmaster—both ardent carbonarios. Someone more important than they must have incited them to commit the act and provided the arms, but the truth has never been known. José de Alpoím, then in Spain, claimed the credit, but he was known to be given to boasting.

The shocking murder of Carlos and his heir-apparent brought Manuel II (1908–1910), an amiable boy of not quite nineteen, to the throne. He had not been expected to inherit, and consequently had received no training for the future duties of kingship. Manuel's understandable confusion was rendered worse by Franco's immediate resignation from office and departure from public life forever. The recent dictator, often called "the last monarchist in Portugal," was really by no means the last, but his resignation left no one to uphold the throne with any vigor, because Hintze had recently died and Castro was superannuated.

A Portuguese historian has thus characterized Manuel: "He was already not the crowned son of a monarch. He was the pallid son of a murdered man. He was not an heir. He was an orphan." [4] The thirty-two months his reign lasted are seen in retrospect as only months of waiting until the Republicans felt ready to take possession of the country.

Several ministries held office during Manuel's brief reign, though they no longer called themselves Progressives and Regenerators and were staffed by men hitherto little known. No one appeared with genuine strength and resolution, and it became evident that the days of monarchy were numbered, even though the Republicans repre- sented a minority in the country. Their strength lay in the cities, how- ever, and it would be Lisbon, not the Trás-os-Montes or the Algarve, that would decide the nation's future.

By October 1910, the Republicans felt ready, and on the third of that month an assassination touched off the revolt. Dr. Miguel Bombarda, an alienist very active in the Republican movement, was fatally shot by one of his own patients. Radical journals and propa- gandists made the most of the incident and declared the killer a royal agent. They struck their blow the following day; violence began when the officers and crews of two warships anchored in the Tagus began to lob shells in the general direction of the Necessidades Palace. António Machado Santos and Luís de Almeida, leaders of the Carbonaria, appeared in the streets directing their followers. The king summoned his officials to the palace, in which several grenades had burst, but only a few appeared. Paiva Couceiro, a loyal monarchist to the last, tried to rally soldiers to Manuel's defense, but could gain no real following.

The king and his mother, Queen Amelia, could do nothing but leave the country, and, after some difficulties, managed to board the royal yacht and sail for Gibraltar, from which a British ship conveyed them to England. In this way the Portuguese monarchy expired after 770 years of existence.

4. João Ameal, *História de Portugal*, p. 752.

16

The Portuguese Republic[1]

REORGANIZATION

The Republicans in Portugal had been opportunistic, with grandiose aspirations for the future but with small idea of how to implement them. Far from proving to be saviors of the country, they found matters going from bad to worse during their regime, which is commonly thought of as lasting from 1910 to 1926, when a new form of government replaced theirs. The monarchy had been in precarious straits during its final decades, but it had at least represented historical continuity, which the republic did not.

The new masters of Portugal could, however, face the future without fear of foreign intervention. Europe was still monarchical with only two other republics, the French and the Swiss, existing in 1910. But Metternich's day of interventions in behalf of princes had long passed; several European thrones were unstable, and continental opinion had grown generally liberal.

The two leading representatives of the Bragança line were now the exiled Manuel and the son of the ruler banished in 1834, who

---

1. There is little good history written about the Portuguese republic. Arthur Ribeiro Lopes in his *Histoire de la République Portugaise*, deals mostly with the last years of monarchy. Jesús Pabón, in *La República Portuguesa*, and Vicente de Bragança-Cunha, *Revolutionary Portugal, 1910–1936*, are extremely conservative.

called himself Miguel II. Soon after the revolution, the two met and agreed that Manuel should be the sole pretender. Although several restoration attempts in Manuel's name took place in the next decade, the king, so far as is known, did not associate himself with them or attempt to return to Portugal. He died childless in early middle life, so, because Miguel had children, the pretendership passed to the junior Bragança branch.

The republic meanwhile named the elderly Teófilo Braga provisional president, pending an election and the adoption of a new constitution. Various changes took place; the flag was remodeled by alteration of the coat of arms and the substitution of green and red bars for the old blue and white. The *escudo* replaced the former *real* as the monetary unit and at first had a high purchasing and exchange value, though it rapidly depreciated as the republic brought inflation.

The Constitution of 1911 provided for a four-year presidency, based more on the pattern of the United States than of France. There was to be a bicameral legislature, consisting of a Senate and a Chamber of Deputies, and a Ministry responsible to both the president and the houses, but chiefly to the former.

Dr. Braga held office until the adoption of the constitution and the election of his successor, Manuel de Arriaga (1839–1917), an old man and compromise candidate, who had been out of political life for years. Arriaga served nearly a full term, thereby establishing almost a record for the republic, whose presidents thereafter usually resigned or were removed by violence. Nine held office for sixteen years, and most of their names are all but forgotten.

In the early years, when the republic seemed to have a chance of succeeding, Prime Minister Afonso Costa (1871–1937) proved the strong man of the Arriaga administration. Costa, the most bitter of Portuguese anticlericals, declared that he could and would extinguish the Roman Catholic Church in the country within two generations. It was a vain and foolish boast, especially because his two generations had to be reduced to the thirteen months he actually spent in office. Costa had undeniable ability, however; a fact admitted by his worst enemies. He made probably the most sincere attempt of any republican statesman to end the yearly deficits, with a law to the effect that once an annual budget had been passed there could be no tampering with it. This proved no more popular with the republican politicians than it would have proved with their monarchist predecessors.

The Church understandably hated Costa, but, in its weakened

condition at the time, it could do little to force him out of office. His downfall came because of labor troubles and the efforts of other politicians, who grew restive because of the number of arrests he made and his generally domineering ways. Demonstrations sponsored by them and pressure brought upon President Arriaga forced him and his ministry from power in February 1914. He left with at least the satisfaction of having passed a law separating Church and State in Portugal.

Shortly before President Arriaga gave way to Bernardino Machado (1851–1944) the First World War broke out and Portugal found it impossible to stay neutral.

WORLD WAR I

When Britain and Germany exchanged declarations of war in August 1914, the Anglo-Portuguese alliance still existed, unaltered by the recent revolution. But, because there seemed no way in which Portugal could be of immediate help, the British did not insist on its participation. Sir Edward Grey, at first, told the Portuguese minister that his government would be satisfied if Portugal merely refrained from declaring neutrality. The Lisbon authorities worried most about Angola and Mozambique, which lay immediately adjacent to the German Southwest and East Africa. German patrols did, in fact, begin to penetrate Portuguese territory, alleging that they sought deserters from their own forces. Unpleasant incidents occurred, and there was fighting on the frontiers of both Angola and Mozambique as a result of German attacks. It appears that the Kaiser's African authorities, rather out of touch with Europe, had the mistaken impression that Portugal had declared war. When they realized their error they expressed regrets and withdrew.

Portugal was nevertheless in the war by February 1916. Grey had finally asked for active participation, because the Portuguese had small arms to spare that England needed and because it could furnish troops to remedy somewhat the Allied manpower shortage on the Western front. Portugal demurred at first, feeling itself unprepared to enter the great conflict, but its feeling rapidly grew anti-German. What finally decided the matter was the presence of many German cargo ships that had been interned in the Tagus since the outbreak of war. England needed ships badly, and Grey asked Portugal to commandeer these, promising to buy them and award Portuguese firms contracts for their refitting. The Machado government complied and a Portuguese commandant took possession of the vessels on February 24, 1916. Germany, followed by Austria-Hungary, issued a declaration of war.

Portugal now took stock of its slender resources to see what it could do economically and militarily to aid the war effort. A Franco-English military mission came to Portugal, where stepped-up training went on. In January 1917, 25,000 men were ready to be sent to France under the command of General Fernando Tamagnini de Abreu e Silva, a number later increased to 40,000. At the same time, Portugal reinforced its troops in Africa, where German colonial resistance to Allied forces did not cease until after the Armistice.

It appears that the Portuguese soldiers sent to France had not been properly trained or psychologically prepared for what they were to face. The British awarded them a sector in Flanders between the Lys River and its tributaries, and as long as the Germans refrained from a serious attack, they held their part of the front. But when Erich Ludendorff launched the great spring offensive of 1918, one of the first sectors struck was the Lys, where a Portuguese division was surprised and overwhelmed. The neighboring British also suffered heavily and barely managed to avoid a collapse of the front. The Portuguese took little part in the remaining operations and General Tamagnini suffered harsh criticism, though his subordinate, Manuel Gomes da Costa emerged as a national hero.

Sidónio Pais had meanwhile overthrown Bernardino Machado and taken the Portuguese presidency himself at the end of 1917. Pais, though often seen in uniform, was no soldier but a former cabinet minister who had also represented Portugal at Berlin before the declaration of war. Handsome, and especially popular with Portuguese women, he owed office largely to military support and scarcely bothered, during the year he governed, to conceal the fact that he was a dictator; precursor, as some have called him, of the "New State" presently initiated by Salazar.

Pais began his term with a stirring proclamation appealing to Portuguese patriotism in support of the war effort, but his own performance failed to live up to his words. He showed lethargy in answering appeals for reinforcements by the army in France, and paid more attention to home politics than to the war. If he had an economic program over and above his vague promises to laborers, his life and dictatorship proved too short for any achievement. Though he staged and won an election of sorts for the presidency, this was mainly because no other candidates presented themselves. The popularity he had gained by his glibness and personality began to fade, and by the Armistice of November 11, 1918, there had been plots against him and abortive risings. Finally, a month after the Armistice, as Pais was about to board a train at Lisbon for Oporto, a young fanatic of feeble intellect dealt him a mortal wound with a pistol. Arrested and questioned by the police, the youth admitted that he knew little or nothing about Pais and mainly wanted the notoriety of having slain the chief of state. For some reason, he was not executed and presently regained liberty, though he later died in a lunatic asylum.

THE FINAL MONARCHIST ATTEMPT

Paiva Couceiro, who had never wavered in allegiance to the Braganças, had gone into exile following the downfall of Manuel II. In both 1911 and 1912, he had conducted small expeditions into northern Portugal from Spanish Galicia, in hopes of starting a popular rising in behalf of monarchy. He had failed in both attempts and had temporarily given up and come to terms with the republicans, who allowed him to return to the country.

He had not abandoned hope, however, and bided his time until he felt the Portuguese had grown disillusioned with the republic. Sidónio Pais had briefly been nearly a monarch, and the people had not noticeably objected. His successor in the presidency, Admiral João de Canto e Castro, was not a strong figure, and the year 1919 might well be the opportune one.

Couceiro began a revolt in northern Portugal and, having won over various garrisons there, proclaimed the restored monarchy on January 19, 1919. Other soldiers went over to him, and the cities of Viana do Castelo, Braga, Guimarães, Oporto, Bragança, Vila Real, Lamego, and Viseu raised the royal standard. The western end of the River Vouga marked the frontier between the Portuguese Republic of the south and the short-lived Portuguese Monarchy of the north. Part of the Lisbon garrison pronounced for the king, and Aires de Ornelas, an old Africa hand with a reputation nearly equal to Paiva's own, went over to the monarchists.

Yet the movement collapsed as quickly as it had begun. Most of the Lisbon forces remained republican and defeated the royalists as they advanced to Monsanto near the capital. Northern Portugal soon came under government control again, and the leaders of the insurrection took to flight. Many were captured, though Couceiro escaped to go into exile again. Over a decade later, the Salazar regime permitted him to return to Portugal, where he died of old age in 1944. There were to be other uprisings in the country before the end of the republic, but none in behalf of the Braganças, whose cause was apparently dead.

The Republic's Last Years

The Portuguese Republic passed through its worst period between World War I and 1926. Of four presidents within eight years, only one completed his four-year term. In 1920, the nation had four ministries, one lasting twenty-four hours and another six days. A revolutionary military junta in 1921 forced President António de Almeida, practically at pistol point, to dismiss an unpopular minister, António Granjo, who was then seized and murdered by a rioting mob. The next year Almeida and his adherents were forced to flee to the suburb of Cascais from a revolutionary outbreak until troops could be brought from the provinces to restore order. The *escudo*, meanwhile, dropped to a low never reached before and became worth five cents in terms of United States money.

The president following Almeida, Manuel Teixeira Gomes, was perhaps emboldened to take office because he had been absent for years as Portuguese Ambassador in London and out of touch with domestic politics. He resigned after two years of strikes, military mutinies, short-lived cabinets, and attacks by the press. In 1925, Bernardino Machado, who had tried the presidency once before, risked it a second time. He soon had cause to repent of his courage, because he found himself in the middle of the worst financial scandal in Portuguese history; one that surely cannot be matched in the annals of many nations.

The Bank of Portugal, because of the increase of currency in circulation, had grown accustomed to employing foreign commercial firms to print its banknotes, one of which, Waterlow and Sons Ltd. of London, had fulfilled such a contract in 1922. Two years later, Sir William Waterlow, head of the firm, was hoodwinked by a group of Portuguese swindlers, headed by a Dutchman who presented forged credentials, into using the former plates to print and deliver to them notes amounting to 100 million escudos, supposedly for use in Angola. The Dutchman showed what passed for a letter from the director of the Bank of Portugal, on the strength of which Waterlow innocently allowed the bogus notes to leave his hands. They were soon smuggled into Portugal, where a suspiciously large amount of new currency began appearing in circulation.

The Portuguese conspirators took advantage of the loose banking laws of their country to gain permission to start their own bank, the Angola e Metropole, which opened its doors in Oporto in July 1925. Meanwhile, again through their Dutch agent, they had obtained an even larger printing of notes from the gullible Waterlow. What finally tripped the swindlers was, first, the sudden affluence of men "without visible means," and, second, the discovery that some notes bore numbers duplicating those already in circulation. A rapid investigation led to the closing of the Banco Angola e Metropole and numerous arrests. The government, not yet knowing how much false currency existed, made the courageous decision to honor all the bogus notes and withdraw them from circulation. It took this step to prevent public panic as the facts became known and to avoid paralysis of business transactions.[2]

The Bank of Portugal commenced a suit against the Waterlow firm in an English court in 1930, which went finally, after several appeals, to the House of Lords. The bank received an award of £610,392 damages on the grounds that the illicit notes and their redemption had seriously impaired its own privilege of note issue.[3]

The effect on Portugal of the large-scale fraud is hard to measure, but it certainly caused confidence in the government and the national bank to fall. Portuguese with a knowledge of the world knew that in most countries such a swindle would have been detected immediately. The Minister of Finance had permitted the Banco Angola e Metropole to be chartered after insufficient investigation and let its transactions continue for five months. The whole affair had been nationally humiliating and had certainly given support to those tired of an inept republic and hoping for something more efficient.

2. Full details of this case are furnished by Sir Cecil H. Kisch, *The Portuguese Bank Note Case. The Story and Solution of a Financial Perplexity.*
3. *Ibid.*, p. v.

17

Carmona and Salazar

By early 1926, the Portuguese Republic had ceased to command respect abroad or confidence at home. It had fallen politically into a near anarchy that existing institutions and practices showed no sign of ending. Of its respected founders, Braga was dead; Machado, though again president, had reached the age of seventy-five. The bank-note crisis had furnished the last straw for many; the republic had had its chance and failed, and it was now time to try something else. The army was the one institution in the country able to bring about a change that stood any chance of being constructive. Recent precedents in Europe could not fail to influence the Portuguese. Benito Mussolini's semi-military regime had been in power in Italy for nearly four years and seemed to have corrected a rather chaotic situation there. Miguel Primo de Rivera (1870–1930) of Spain furnished the main inspiration, however, for in 1923, by military *coup d'état*, he had seized power to bolster the sagging monarchy of Alfonso XIII. Spanish soldiers possessed an ingrained habit that Portuguese troops shared; they would follow their officers and obey any orders to support or overthrow a regime.

The name of General Manuel Gomes da Costa (1863–1929) began to appear most prominently among officers discontented with the government. He was rather old for what he intended to do, but

142

he had a talent for rhetoric that many found appealing. António de Oliveira Salazar (1889–1970), a youngish professor in the Faculty of Law at Coimbra and a known conservative, had acquired some reputation as an economist, and da Costa privately conferred with him at Braga on May 26. All that is known of this interview is that Salazar expounded his own philosophy of government, which was as much religious as political. The general then went to an arranged meeting with about a hundred officers of the 11th regiment of cavalry and the 8th and 29th of infantry, and won them to his cause. He sent two as emissaries to the local division commander, General Gomes Peres, who are reported as saying to him: "If you will come and take part with us in the national and republican movement we are about to undertake, we shall have the greatest honor to serve under your orders; if not, we shall obey only General Gomes da Costa." [1] Peres refused, and the conspirators allowed him to leave. He then tried to rouse the national republican guard against the officers, to no effect.

Gomes da Costa had meanwhile planned two marches on Lisbon; a northern one led by himself from Braga, and a southern one from Évora under General António Oscar de Fragoso Carmona. For his own march to the capital, Gomes selected a force of 400 young men, with no artillery and only two machine guns, though he planned to have a reserve column in case of need. His eloquent proclamation to the country was delivered on May 28, 1926:

> Portuguese: For men of dignity and honor the situation of the country is intolerable. Bowed low beneath the tyranny of a licentious minority, the shamed nation feels itself dying. For myself, I openly revolt! And let men of courage and dignity come with me, arms in hand, if they want, as I do, to conquer or die. And I cry, "to arms, Portugal!" [2]

Lisbon learned of the rising in the small hours of May 28, and a crowd assembled at the Rossio railroad station, where manifestos were being circulated from a Committee of Public Safety. These made numerous demands; first for the salvation of the republic and next for correction of various grievances, nearly all of which were remedied by Salazar years later.

Oporto went over to the insurrection, which triumphed with very little fighting. Gomes da Costa entered the northern city to great

1. Jacques Ploncard d'Assac, *Salazar*, p. 41.
2. João Ameal, *História de Portugal*, p. 784.

applause, and President Bernardino Machado invited Naval Commander José Mendes Cabeçadas to form a ministry. This officer was part of the da Costa movement but of the far-left wing, and Machado evidently chose him in hopes of saving his own administration. On May 31, the Senate and Chamber of Deputies held their last meeting, with only a few attending. Machado now saw that he could not remain president and consequently resigned and left the palace at Belem. Cabeçadas went to Coimbra for a conference with Gomes, in which they ostensibly came to agreement.[3]

A few monarchist journals left in Portugal might have been expected to press for a royal restoration but they refrained from doing so, because it was apparent that da Costa and Cabeçadas had no such thought in mind. The royalists, therefore, limited themselves to asking for as conservative a regime as possible, closely allied to the interest of the Church, appreciating that, though the Portuguese wanted stability, they did not want a king.

The accord between Gomes and Cabeçadas had been only superficial, for they represented two very different points of view. When the latter returned to Lisbon he named a ministry in which three men held all the offices. He appointed himself President of the Council and Minister of Marine, Justice, and Religion. Gomes was given the portfolios for War, the Colonies, and Agriculture. A third member of the triumvirate, General Ochoa, was given charge of Foreign Affairs. When Gomes learned of the assignments, he exclaimed: "You see I'm Minister of Agriculture, to busy myself with potatoes. I'm not *going to* Lisbon; I'm *marching on* Lisbon." [4]

Still, he and Cabeçadas held another conference before the march took place. There was a reshuffling of offices in which General Ochoa gave way to General Carmona in Foreign Affairs, Cabeçadas kept the presidency of the Council and Ministership of the Interior, and Gomes da Costa, relieved of potatoes, retained War and the Colonies.

Salazar's First Ministry

Gomes da Costa had been impressed with Salazar at their recent meeting and wished him named Minister of Finance. The triumvirs knew that finance was by far the knottiest problem facing Portugal

3. d'Assac, p. 44.
4. *Ibid.*, p. 45.

and that they, with their military backgrounds, did not understand it at all. When first offered the portfolio, Salazar declined, saying privately that the generals and commander assumed that professors knew everything, which was manifestly untrue. He later said that he refused because of the wide gulf separating the intellectual from the man of action. Nevertheless, when they renewed with insistence, he came to Lisbon, where he was minister for five days. He then resigned and left, with the plausible excuse that his aged mother, Maria do Resgate Salazar, lay at the point of death at Santa Comba, the family home. However, the five days gave him an opportunity to learn something of the state of Portuguese finances—enough to enable him to write of them before taking up their reform in earnest.

He sent a letter to the ministers by a Coimbra student; a lecture of sorts to da Costa in which the main advice was to get rid of Cabeçadas, not because Salazar doubted his honesty and sincerity but because his "constitutional prejudices" stood in the way of genuine reform. The letter was read aloud in cabinet meeting, and, as it was heard, several present broke in demanding that the student not be allowed to finish. Gomes insisted that they must hear it out, saying that all points of view merited consideration. He continued:

> I know some are trying to push me into a dictatorship, but this will not happen. Intrigue shall not succeed in annulling the efforts of those who have begun this work. Doubts should be set at rest. I repeat loudly that I do not want to be a dictator. They speak of Primo de Rivera and Mussolini, but they had the forces of monarchs to aid them, the principle of supreme authority that monarchs represent. A military dictator in Portugal would create the impression of taking possession of Portugal as his personal property. There is no king in Portugal. I am only a soldier.[5]

Gomes da Costa seemed to feel that a march on Lisbon was the indispensable prelude to implementation of his nebulous program, so he entered the capital on June 6 with a few troops, whose arrival did not furnish much of a spectacle. The press, meanwhile, announced that he would become president of the republic. For a few days the populace waited to see what would happen, only to find nothing happening.

5. *Ibid.*, p. 48.

CARMONA

When it became evident that da Costa, in spite of his march on Lisbon, was going to accomplish little and was afraid to take decisive steps, the civilian politicians began to reform their ranks. Meanwhile, Cabeçadas resigned from the government, and da Costa, temporarily absent from the city, returned and took over full powers *de facto*. But he had little time to exercise them, even had he known how, for his bubble of prestige had already burst, and on July 7 he was arrested and deposed by General Carmona. He exclaimed angrily to his successor: "Yesterday you swore fidelity to me and today you demolish me. I do not understand." What he needed to understand was that, however useful he had been in May, he had become expendable in July. He found himself deported to the Azores, where, in September he was both promoted to field marshal and given a pension. In this way Carmona got a useless but troublesome man out of the way and at the same time honored him for overthrowing a regime for which he had no substitute to offer. Later judged harmless, da Costa was allowed back in Portugal and given one or two ornamental but innocuous missions until his death in 1929.

Carmona was a better soldier and an abler man than da Costa, but his military background scarcely fitted him to grapple with Portugal's most urgent problems. He had once served in a cabinet as Minister of War and had later been given the responsibility of prosecuting a group of officers who had taken part in a rising in 1925. Rather surprisingly, he asked the court for their acquittal, saying: "If we see the authors of the evils from which the country is suffering travelling at large abroad, while here men of such great civic virtue are branded as criminals, there must be something wrong. . . . The country is sick. . . ." [6] The statement well illustrates his habits of thought; he despised civilian politicians and believed in the army as the one national institution above politics and able to furnish leadership without regard to personal interest. To say, as one author does, that he hardly knew a credit from a debit is to exaggerate, but Carmona was no more of an economist than Gomes.

During the two years he governed before Salazar's advent, he had times of rough going, because this revolution, like its predecessor

6. Hugh Kay, *Salazar and Modern Portugal*, p. 36.

of 1910, proved slow in bringing Utopia and soon led to disillusion-ment. In the course of 1927, risings occurred in Oporto and Lisbon. The Oporto revolt collapsed only after the loss of many lives; the Lisbon one proved still more difficult to control. Carmona placed the capital in a state of siege, and when he had quelled the insurrec-tion, during which government planes bombed the revolters, he sent 600 persons into exile overseas.

From 1926 to 1928, General João José Sinel de Cordes filled the office of Finance Minister to the best of his limited ability. He felt that Portugal needed a foreign loan of £12 million and sent General Ivens Ferraz to Geneva to request it of the League of Nations. The League representatives responded favorably but imposed the condi-tion that an agent of theirs be appointed to oversee Portuguese state finances and examine the Bank of Portugal. Because this would amount virtually to loss of national sovereignty, Ferraz, however great his country's economic problems, could only refuse.[7]

Minister Cordes also tried diplomacy to bring about a reduction of Portugal's considerable debt to Great Britain. Negotiation with the English Chancellor of the Exchequer, Winston Churchill, scaled down the obligation to £24 million, but Portugal proved unable to pay even this moderate amount.[8]

Carmona so badly needed help in the Finance Department that his thoughts turned to Salazar of Coimbra. A month after being elected president of the nation in March 1928, he persuaded the pro-fessor to accept the financial portfolio. During their first conversation following his appointment, Salazar told the president: "The Portu-guese people have not the patience to await anything for long. If we do not balance the budget quickly, they will not believe us in any-thing." He went on to say that he would balance it within a year. Carmona replied: "They told me that you were a professor absorbed in his calling and completely strange to the realities of life. If I so believed, this brief conversation has just enlightened me. No one can be a stranger to the realities of life when he has so vast and complete a knowledge of the popular psychology." [9]

The day had not yet arrived when Salazar would be the ruler of Portugal and Carmona the figurehead. The general-president was far from a nobody; he still commanded the army, and on this command

7. *Ibid.*, p. 30.
8. *Ibid.*
9. d'Assac, p. 58.

everything, for a time, depended. All Salazar was being asked to do was to manage finances, and at the beginning he had no physical power whatever at his call and he lived under the protection of Carmona and the army.

EARLY LIFE OF SALAZAR

António de Oliveira Salazar was born at Santa Comba Dão, near Coimbra, on April 29, 1889. His father, António de Oliveira, who lived to be ninety-three and died in 1932, was an estate manager for a wealthy landowner. His mother, Maria do Resgate Salazar, died in 1926 at the age of eighty. Although extremely religious, she was a practical woman and ran a cantina concession at the nearby Vimieiro railroad station. From Salazar's later remarks, it seems that the mother exercised more influence over him during his childhood and later than the father. There were other children, the most important being Maria, who, like her brother, never married and during his years as dictator kept house for him and managed his practical affairs.

The boy first went to school at Santa Comba Dão and later at Vimieiro, and at eleven entered the seminary at Viseu. He appears to have been noted for indifference to athletics, which the school permitted, and for complete obedience to all rules, which the other boys violated whenever possible. He remained at Viseu until 1909, and in 1905 began theological studies, in which he showed greatest interest in the writings of Thomas Aquinas. He took minor orders in 1908, and for a short time preached in the neighboring parish church. His next logical step would have been to be ordained priest, but he finally refrained, feeling that he could be of greater service to the Church as a layman.

In preparation for Coimbra University, he studied for a time at the College of Via Sacra in Viseu, which was modern in outlook and given to new teaching methods, largely imported from England. Via Sacra required pupils to give public discourses, and Salazar delivered his first in December 1909. He spoke of the need to change the people of Portugal, and advocated education as a cure for their faults. Too many talked about popular enlightenment, he said, and too few did anything about it.

He registered in law at Coimbra in 1910 and soon afterward Manuel II was overthrown and Portugal became a republic. Revolutionists invaded the University Faculty of Theology, smashing furniture, mutilating portraits of kings, and tearing professorial robes. Salazar here took the only youthful part he ever assumed in politics when he was named part of a delegation to go to Lisbon and protest such wantonly destructive tactics. As between monarchy and republic, he seemed to be indifferent, or at least took no open stand; his main interests lay in the welfare of the Church and popular education as a remedy for Portugal's ills. His party affiliation was Christian-Democratic, with heavy emphasis on Christian, meaning Catholic.

He took the bachelor's degree at Coimbra in November 1914, at the mature age of twenty-five, because he had entered when older than most students. His record is described as especially brilliant. Salazar now exhibited the one romantic attachment ever known of him. He asked the hand of his father's employer's daughter in marriage, but was refused on the grounds that the young man, however intellectual, was poor and had no future. The girl married someone else and Salazar remained single through life, but it is probably wrong to conclude, as some do, that he never recovered from this disappointment in love.

He worked for the doctorate and gained it in 1918, but already, a year earlier, he had been appointed Assistant Professor to the Chair of Economic Sciences at Coimbra. By the time of achieving the doctorate, Salazar had written two theses, one on stockbrokerage in gold and the other on the problems of wheat production. As a teacher, he became so well known and so influential with students that many even not enrolled in his classes often went to hear him. At Coimbra, Salazar shared living quarters for thirteen years with Manuel Gonçalves Cerejeira, a teaching priest who later became Cardinal-Patriarch of Lisbon. The two young men exercised a considerable influence on each other, and many years afterward the Cardinal said to an interviewer:

Salazar did his best for a long time to put some order into my character and my writings. And I never stopped taking him to task for his punctuality and sense of personal discipline which seemed to me exaggerated. "You are a creature of habit," I would cry out impatiently, when I happened to look inside his closet which was neater than a young girl's, or when he left for his daily walk at the appointed hour.[10]

10. Christine Garnier, *Salazar in Portugal: An Intimate Portrait*, pp. 158–59.

When the royalist rising under Paiva Couceiro took place in 1919, Salazar had no part in it, but his known conservative sympathies caused him, with three colleagues, to be accused of complicity, and all were suspended from the university while an investigation of their activities was opened. Salazar and the other three had no difficulty in proving that they had abstained from politics, and all were exonerated. The 1919 rising had been an almost entirely military affair conducted by soldiers, and Salazar had failed the physical examination when earlier called for army service.

In 1921, Salazar consented to be a candidate for the côrtes on the Catholic-Center ticket to represent Guimarães. He was elected and on September 2 took his seat in Lisbon as a deputy. That very evening he went back to Coimbra and resigned from the office. He gave no precise reasons, but it is believed that he found Portuguese parliamentary politics, as then practiced, highly distasteful. He nevertheless kept his standing in the Catholic-Center and made a notable speech to a party congress in Lisbon in 1922. Pope Benedict XV had recently advocated that Portuguese Catholics accept the Republican regime, and Salazar, in his address, showed no objections, but did say that public sovereignty had its origin with God: *non est potestas nisi a Deo*. He felt that the Christian idea properly was that of a society not egalitarian but hierarchical and considered this necessary for the attainment of man's ends. The Church, he contended, accepted the historic differences between forms of government and recognized the full right of peoples to choose their kind of political organization, subject to (1) the full right of Catholics, if not in control, to prefer speculatively this or that form of government; (2) full liberty to embrace a newly constituted regime; (3) liberty to obey, in the name of common welfare, and in the name of peace, constituted governments and, *a fortiori*, legitimate ones; and (4) interdiction of sedition and rebellion, except in rare cases.

Salazar's problem was to reconcile the idea of a hierarchical, and hence nondemocratic, society with that of a democratic regime. He was here attempting almost the impossible, but he tried, saying that although the policy of the Church and that of the State could not be the same in all matters, the former could require of the State the most favorable conditions for the carrying out of its divine mission. When functioning as a State, people could act independently of the Church, *except* that they must never depart from its moral principles.

In another part of the discourse, he departed from the purely religious question by saying that the "isolated individual" had grown obsolete and that the time would soon come when men, in interest groups, needed to act in unison. This was political thinking, and a clear foreshadowing of the totalitarian corporate state system he would one day put into effect in Portugal.

In the two years between the five-day ministry of 1926 and the acceptance of office under Carmona, Salazar made one of his few visits to foreign parts, to France and Belgium. He enjoyed France and while there made a pious pilgrimage to the shrine at Lourdes. Nearly thirty years later, long after the bitter French experience in World War II, he praised France, recalling its beauty and culture.

THE FIRST YEARS OF OFFICE

By the time Salazar published his first budget, August 1, 1928, he had become the leading person in the government, though not yet the most powerful. He still depended on Carmona and the army for continuance in office, and he had severe critics from the outset. On June 9, a few weeks after assuming the ministry, he visited the general army headquarters in Lisbon to thank the officers for kind remarks they had made about him. In a brief address, he said:

It is natural that some among you should have had curiosity to see the Minister of Finance. Here he is and you see him; he is a very humble person. He has precarious health and is never sick; he has a limited capacity for work and works without ceasing. How is this miracle possible? Because many good souls in Portugal pray that he may remain in that place. I represent a principle; that of a policy of truth and sincerity opposed to a policy of lies and secrecy.[11]

Appearances such as these were rare however, because Salazar customarily shunned the limelight. He left to Carmona the tasks of presiding over public gatherings and laying cornerstones. The exact nature of his relations with the president seems not precisely known; they were both strong personalities and doubtless had their disagreements, but none of this appeared to the public. Salazar once offered his resignation when Carmona wished to limit Portugal's too-numerous religious festivals; his objections carried the day and the resignation was withdrawn. His responsibilities widened and in 1930 the

11. d'Assac, p. 60.

Ministries of the Interior and the Colonies were added to his financial responsibilities. Nevertheless, the writer recalls, from personal conversations, that in 1930 Portugal still thought of President-General Carmona as the ruler of the country.

18

The New State

SALAZAR IN FULL POWER

The Salazar regime will be as diversely judged by historians as that of Pombal two centuries earlier, but the bitterest detractor of the professor-dictator will not deny that he gave Portugal the only smoothly functioning government it had seen in a century and a quarter. Four years after accepting the financial post from Carmona, he took full charge of the administration when the president appointed him head of the Council of Ministers, an office he held until his physical collapse in 1968. Carmona, already sixty-three, had come to know the abilities of his quiet subordinate and thereafter gracefully accepted the status of a figurehead.

Salazar had first taken office as an inexperienced specialist in balancing budgets, and his reports thereafter regularly pronounced them balanced. Just how he accomplished the balancing will not be learned from his occasional speeches and communications to the legislature and people, for these are filled with platitudinous philosophy and lacking in concrete details. He inevitably raised taxes and cut all expenses possible, but he could not have saved enough by such measures, because he spent large amounts modernizing the armed forces. One of his Portuguese detractors—living abroad—charged that Salazar counted loans as revenue, which, if true, amounted to a less than frank approach to the problem. He created much employment by undertaking a program of improvements to add to the nation's network of roads and to stimulate farm production. Portugal already had a railroad system adequate to its needs, but Salazar improved the roadbeds and the service. He encouraged growth in the building trades, especially by the construction of new housing for workers. By the end of 1933, registered unemployment had sunk to less than one percent of the laborers. Emigration declined, though it certainly rose again later in Salazar's life. Despite all the known facts and statistics, his financial methods had and still have some aura of mystery about them.

Salazar administered economically; he planned little. He improved what existed but innovated only slightly; he was attached to the Portuguese society in which he had lived and desired no fundamental alterations. He had no enthusiasm for industrialization and saw it as a breeder of discontent and potential trouble among the masses. He resented the economic subjugation of Portugal to foreigners and took some steps to end it; for ready cash he bought out the foreign-owned telephone lines. In the necessary development of hydroelectric power, he was careful that the production should be Portuguese-owned, without foreign attachments. Most of his reforms for increasing the comforts and amenities of life were concentrated in Lisbon, which became an island of luxury in a sea of national poverty. In its possession of automobiles, telephones, and medical practitioners, the capital attained figures out of proportion to the rest of the country. The assertion that Salazar froze Portugal to the extent possible in the mold he knew is generally true.

His watchwords in other matters were conservatism and a constant emphasis on the virtues of patriotism. An example is the funeral he arranged for Manuel II, born five months earlier than himself, who died in 1932 at the age of forty-three. The former king had terminated a brief reign a generation earlier; Salazar had just commenced a long one of his own. It was not monarchist sentiment that made the dictator invite Britain, where the king had died, to send his body to Portugal for burial in the Bragança family vault. He wished to remind the people of their links with the past, far removed from republicanism and democracy. Salazar spoke at the interment and, instead of correctly calling Manuel a boy king wholly unable to cope with a complicated situation, he termed him a great man unjustly banished from a country toward which he never afterward felt resentment.[1]

SALAZAR'S MIND

During the dictator's life and administration, he was often depicted as a more subtle and complex person than the truth warranted; actually, his ideas were exactly what he professed them to be. Three principles dominated his thinking and action; belief in the Catholic Religion, distrust of popular government, and abhorrence of communism. Most Portuguese would have agreed with the first and third sentiments, and a large, though uncertain, number with the second. Salazar at one time admired Mussolini, whose concordat with the papacy and establishment of the Catholic Church in Italy in 1929 pleased him. He is said to have kept the *duce*'s picture on his desk for years and to have removed it only when he became the obvious lackey of Hitler. His admiration for Italian fascism had limitations, however, for Mussolini at times seemed more pagan than Christian and had some disreputable characters as associates. Salazar disapproved of the duce's spectacular costumes and his habit of orating to mobs to the accompaniment of roars of animal-like applause.

He disapproved of Hitler, whom he never met but considered a useful barrier against Russian communism. The dislike grew when the *führer* began to demand colonies for Germany, and when rumors spread of appeasing him with Angola and Mozambique. Salazar was no imperialist in the sense of wishing to add to what Portugal already had, but he never thought of relinquishing any national possession.

Portuguese have generally admired England politically because of its stability and the restraint and self-discipline of the British people. Salazar shared this feeling but saw no hope of transplanting Anglo-Saxon institutions to his own country. Portugal had tried that in the days of the Progressives and Regenerators, and the experiment had failed dismally. Moreover, Salazar had growing doubts of England as the 1930s passed, for he thought he saw that nation becoming self-indulgent and unwilling to accept the challenge offered by the mighty and growing Nazi war machine. He read the future more accurately than did either Stanley Baldwin or Neville Chamberlain, his English opposite numbers.

1. Jacques d'Assac, *Salazar*, p. 75.

His hatred of communism was mixed with a certain amount of puzzlement. For all his conservatism, he was liberal in some ways and believed in freedom of thought and freedom of conscience. He could not understand, in the 1930s, why so many enlightened liberals idealized Russia and defended all its actions, because those were the years of the Stalin purges, with the accompanying mass executions, imprisonments, transportations, and other features of Genghis-Khan socialism.

Yet, for all his belief in human dignity, Salazar felt that political necessity sometimes warranted firm measures, even the incarceration or exile of opponents of his own regime. If, at times, his police were rougher than he would have been himself, he had to conclude that they knew their business and let them operate in their own way. "Half the country was illiterate, and an easy prey to unscrupulous campaigners, and if there was anything that Salazar hated most, it was the irresponsible manipulation of untutored public opinion for political ends." [2] Portugal had had an overdose of this in the final monarchical and republican years, and he meant to end it, because nothing good could come from political demagogues.

> Salazar began his adult life with the intention of becoming a priest of the Church. But somehow he was deflected into administration and government. But he remained, in his single-minded devotion to what he thought was his task and his duty, . . . a priest. He centered everything on himself—all politics, initiative, even thought, were frozen. He demanded and got complete unquestioning obedience and in return he promised the people of Portugal salvation.[3]

He worked unceasingly and rarely took vacations. "The state does not pay me to lead a social life," he said; "it pays me to spend my time solving its vital problems." [4]

THE CONSTITUTION OF THE NEW STATE

On March 19, 1933, Salazar submitted the constitution on which he and others had worked for months to a national referendum. Of the 1,214,159 registered voters in Portugal, 719,160 opted for it, 5,955

2. Hugh Kay, *Salazar and Modern Portugal*, p. 72.
3. Private letter from Lisbon.
4. Christine Garnier, *Salazar in Portugal*, p. 12.

voted against it, and nearly 500,000 abstained. Portuguese abstentions can mean one of several things: forgetfulness, total ignorance of the issue, indifference, or refusal to vote as a form of protest. No one knows how much each of these reasons counted, but the number of abstentions made the victory of the constitution seem far from overwhelming. From all available evidence, the election was free, though evidence indicates that some later elections Salazar held were not.

There was nothing fixed and final about this constitution—Salazar left the way open for amendments, of which several were later made. By it, Portugal was designated the *Estado Novo* (New State). The governmental system was presidential in theory, with the head of the nation—in this case Carmona—being elected by universal suffrage for seven years. The national head was then empowered to appoint the president of the council—in this case Salazar. The council president could advise the president of the nation on whom to appoint as the other ministers and when to discharge them. The national president had the authority to dissolve the national assembly, but in this, as in other acts, he needed the countersignature of the president of the council besides that of the minister in whose department the act fell. A council of state existed to advise the chief executive, as in monarchical times. It consisted of the president of the council, the presiding officers of both legislative bodies, the president of the supreme court of justice, the attorney general, and ten members at large appointed by the titular executive of the country.

The new legislature consisted of two houses, a national assembly with some resemblance to the old côrtes, chosen popularly, and a corporative chamber, consisting of representatives of corporations, meaning occupational groups and including labor unions. Voters consisted of all male Portuguese citizens able to read and write, but illiterates might have the franchise if they paid a tax of 100 escudos, a sum equivalent to three dollars, though with a higher purchasing power. Women could vote if able to read and write and pay 200 escudos of taxes. Salazar's successor, Caetano, liberalized the election laws and gave the ballot to all adult literate citizens, regardless of sex, who had no criminal records.

The territorial structure of Portugal, with its division into provinces, remained unchanged.

Today the world is full of constitutions that say one thing and mean another, and Portugal's, despite its details and the numerous officials it provided, was carefully rigged to give Salazar and whoever might follow him the supreme power, subject to no veto save that of possible revolution. If a generalization can be made about the government under the dictator, it is that organizational democracy replaced individual democracy, to the extent that the word democracy applies at all. It is worth noting that organized labor was able to speak with a more decisive voice than had ever previously been true through its membership in the corporative chamber.

THE SPANISH CIVIL WAR

Alfonso XIII of Spain had been deposed in 1931 by an election in which not all the votes were counted. The republic that followed grew steadily more leftist; Communists infiltrated some of the organs of government and disorder in the cities increased. In July 1936 a large part of the Spanish army, led by General Francisco Franco, revolted against the republic and a civil war began that lasted until early in 1939 and resulted in the victory of Franco. The Spanish republican regime under attack was not Communist, but was decidedly leftist, and received some military help from Russia. Far more aid came to Franco from Fascist Italy and Nazi Germany, and Salazar, though having no part in the military operations, took a stand in favor of Franco, to whom he granted recognition in 1938. It was feared, with good reason, that Spanish republicans, if victorious, would seize Portugal, because they would be closely linked with the Soviets. The majority opinion in England and France favored Franco's enemies, and although these countries sent almost no help to the republicans, they vehemently criticized Salazar for siding with the fascists. Salazar and his ministry, besides dreading the spread of communism, were primarily interested in preserving the independence of their own nation. Salazar attempted to convince the British of this, and pointed out to their representatives how dangerous to England a Portugal in Spanish Communist hands would be.

The physical aid Portugal supplied to Franco was rather small. Some Portuguese volunteers, whose exact numbers are unknown and only vaguely estimated, fought on Franco's side, one source placing them as high as 20,000. This is certainly much too large and the Spanish leader himself said only that "several thousand" from Portugal had joined him. The assertion that men were conscripted by the Salazar government to fight in Spain is evidently groundless, for all those who went seem to have been volunteers, and some men from

Portugal joined the republicans. The really important aid Portugal gave Franco was the use of its ports, through which munitions and tanks from Germany easily passed.

A mutiny aboard two Portuguese warships in the Tagus early in the Spanish war, during which the crews imprisoned their officers and prepared to sail to the Mediterranean and join the Spanish republicans, was energetically suppressed. It so alarmed the Salazar government, however, that a decree was immediately issued requiring all military personnel and civil employees of the country to declare allegiance to the New State and disavow communism and other revolutionary ideas. There followed the formation of a Portuguese Legion, not to fight in the Spanish war but to combat communism and disorder at home.

When the Spanish conflict ended in March 1939, Portugal breathed a sigh of relief at having survived, but within seven months a greater conflict began that offered the same dangers in even more threatening form.

World War II [5]

Hitler attacked Poland on September 1, 1939, and crushed it in twenty days. England and France declared war on Germany, but the situation remained fairly quiet in the west until the spring of 1940. It seemed to many that a repetition of World War I might then follow, with British and French facing German soldiers in fortifications and entrenchments and a long stalemate ensuing. But the Germans had taken the lessons of the last war more to heart than had their opponents. The following April they occupied Denmark with no resistance and Norway with only weak opposition. The next month, with new tactics and weapons, they staged a great western offensive in which Holland, Belgium, and France quickly collapsed. Great Britain, for the time, stood alone against Germany, and its future looked doubtful.

Portugal had declared neutrality, which it maintained through the war, but stood no chance of avoiding some forms of involvement. When the war became an Atlantic one, because of German submarine activity and British attempts to combat this menace, the

5. A useful study of Portugal's neutral role in World War II is found in A. H. d'Araújo Howorth's A *Aliança Luso-Británica e a Segunda Guerra Mundial*.

Portuguese Azores, Madeira, and Cape Verde Islands were certain to be factors. In the Far East, Japan had for some years been overrunning coastal China and now, with the fall of France and Holland, it occupied Indo-China and threatened Netherlands India. The Portuguese possessions of Macao and Timor were helpless and indefensible; the Japanese could occupy them at any moment they chose. Great Britain remained an ally of Portugal, but could only think of its own threatened survival, and the isolationist United States then thought mainly of avoiding involvement. During the many months when Hitler seemed the certain victor, helpless mainland Portugal could not afford any steps that might offend him, although it had been abundantly demonstrated that he required no provocation to attack a neutral. Spain's attitude was also doubtful, for Franco owed his position largely to the Rome-Berlin Axis, and might attack England in order to seize Gibraltar.

Portuguese policy through the war consistantly aimed at preserving neutrality and avoiding the physical occupation of itself or any overseas possessions. Meanwhile, the country enjoyed a certain prosperity. Refugees from Axis-occupied nations often wished to embark for England, the United States, or Brazil, and the best route lay through Portugal. Some came well provided, and a few chose to stay in the country, living in luxury hotels in Lisbon or the nearby Estoril resort. All this put additional money in circulation and helped certain classes, though it was an inflation prosperity.

Salazar foresaw an allied victory sooner than any other European statesman except Winston Churchill, and prophesied it even in the darkest days following the fall of France. He knew that the United States would enter the war long before most people in this country read the future correctly. He believed from the beginning that the conflict would be long, though he would have liked to see it short and end by negotiation.

The British alliance still existed, but England never asked Portugal to help militarily, which would have meant nothing in view of Portuguese weakness. Both sides were willing to let Salazar stay neutral, because England needed its neutrality to keep in touch with the continent, and Germany found it equally valuable for communication with the New World.

The United States, after it was attacked and forced into the war, felt less concern than did England for neutral sensibilities. President Roosevelt definitely wanted a base in the Azores to combat German submarines and at his urging, Churchill opened negotiations early in 1943 for such a concession. The British promised Portugal all military aid in their power should Germany attempt retaliation. They began landing equipment and men on the islands in September 1943 and setting up a principal base at Horta. The United States made considerable use of the British facilities, and the toll inflicted by German submarines dropped considerably.

The economic part played by Portugal's African colonies in the war proved important. Angola produced diamonds for industrial use, and for some time most of its supply went to England. Mozambique sent coal, copper, and chromium to the Allies, as well as to South Africa, then still a part of the British Commonwealth. Portugal itself had few minerals to sell to the belligerents, but it did have wolfram and made this available to the Allies. It was equally willing to sell to the Axis, but the Atlantic blockade made the sea route next to impossible and transportation through Spain, whose rail lines were in bad condition because of the recent civil war, was slow and unreliable.

In the Far East, Japan having been a threat from the outbreak of the war, the Portuguese worried about their possessions of Macao and Timor. When Japan entered the conflict on December 7, 1941, it quickly captured Hong Kong, near Macao, which they could have taken without resistance, but left alone because it had no military value and was not suited to be a war base.

Timor, amid the Dutch East Indies, proved a somewhat different matter, and even before Pearl Harbor Salazar's Ambassador in London, Armindo Monteiro, told Foreign Minister Anthony Eden that Portugal would resist any Japanese attack on the Portuguese part of the island. Salazar did, in fact, dispatch troops there, though they could have done little except surrender had they arrived ahead of the Japanese. Shortly after Japan entered the war, a few Dutch and Australian soldiers did land on Timor with the idea of defending it. Because no state of war existed between Portugal and Japan, Salazar indignantly ordered them out, saying that their presence was a violation of Portuguese sovereignty. Events moved too fast for him, however; the Japanese arrived and occupied Timor, their government explaining the seizure as a "liberation" from the unwelcome Australians and Dutchmen. The colony remained in the hands of the Japanese until their surrender in 1945 caused its return to the Portuguese, who continue to hold it.

Salazar was beset in those years by forces he could not control, and however he might protest what he considered violations of Portugal's neutrality or sovereignty, he could only remonstrate and instruct his diplomats abroad to do the same. The position was humiliating and his one way of venting frustration was by making bitter speeches at home. To a Portuguese audience on May 4, 1944, he said: "It becomes constantly more difficult to speak, or at least I find it constantly more difficult because, in the midst of the confusion that currently reigns in the world, the more one says, the less he is sure of being understood." [6]

When peace finally came, no one welcomed it more than the Portuguese dictator, for again his weak nation had survived and emerged without the loss of a kilometer of territory. His message to the Portuguese National Assembly, after the fall of Germany, breathed no spirit of neutrality but showed that he considered Portugal one of the victors:

> The curtain has fallen on the tragedy that Europe has played and lived through, in both the flesh and spirit, during these last ten years. . . . Let us bless the victory! I shall say no more. In this solemn, not to say sacred hour, I feel nothing, I experience nothing but a lively sense of gratitude towards the Divine Providence, and pray that its sacred light may illumine the men responsible for the destinies of the world.[7]

POSTWAR PORTUGAL

Portugal had held a presidential election in 1942, in which Carmona, unopposed, had been selected for the second time under the new constitution, though he had actually been fourteen years in office. Carmona had reached seventy-three, and barring unforeseen events would end his days as titular head of Portugal. More important than the question of which general or elder statesman should hold the rather meaningless office of president was that of Portugal's membership in the United Nations Organization. When it was formed, several countries with former fascist associations, including both Spain and Portugal, were left out at Russia's insistence. The Soviet Union, for some time thereafter, regularly vetoed requests for Portuguese admission sponsored by the United States. Not until 1955 did Portugal gain a seat, as part of a compromise between Russia and the

6. d'Assac, *Salazar*, p. 202.
7. *Ibid.*, pp. 205–7.

West whereby sixteen new nations came in. "Salazar was under no illusions about this. Khrushchev, he would wryly say, was the only foreign statesman who understood him: understood, that is, that Salazar had seen through Khrushchev." [8]

The status of Goa and the other Portuguese Indian enclaves began to come under fire, especially after 1947, when Britain left India and France gave up its small possessions there. The Portuguese contended that these distant territories were not colonies but "Overseas Portugal"; an assertion supported by the fact that they had long been officially called "*Ultramar*." Hence, when Britain, France, and Belgium began liquidating their colonial empires, Portugal felt under no obligation to do the same, because its Goa, Diu, and Damão had been acquired in the early sixteenth century. Since that time, the Portuguese argued, these places, as well as those they held in Africa, had become so completely a part of the home country that Portugal was not a colonial power. Such a contention could be ruled well-based or groundless as the foreign observer wished, but in general both the informed and the uninformed saw it as a specious argument for avoiding the general European policy of exodus.

Angola began to be disturbed at the end of 1959, and the movement then started for independence was called a "nationalist" insurrection. There is really no such thing as Angolan nationalism, though there was a wish to throw off white Portuguese control. Angola is a conglomeration of tribes and societies, of which color is the only unifying factor; in its present form it was put together, as were most of the European African possessions, in the 1880s and 1890s, without regard to anything but the faulty maps then existing and the aspirations of European powers. Portugal, the founder of the first empire, had placed the largest number of its own people in Africa. There was thus a society of Portuguese whites in Angola that, having been there for generations or centuries, regarded Africa as its home and had aspirations, if not altogether of independence, at least of more self-determination in the Portuguese world. Mozambique began to feel the same aspirations as Angola, but by the early 1970s neither had separated nor realized its ambitions, white or native.

In 1961 occurred the remarkable episode of Captain Henrique Galvão and an intrepid group of liberal Portuguese, Spanish, and

8. Kay, p. 183.

Spanish-American followers. Galvão, a former official connected with Angola, did not wish to destroy the Portuguese empire but hoped to start a liberal revolution in Angola, mostly engineered by whites, that would spread to Portugal and ultimately to Spain. In sober reality, because the small band could not hope to overcome the Angolan authorities, the real aim may have been publicity for the cause. Galvão and his confederates hijacked the Portuguese luxury liner *Santa Maria*, loaded with passengers, in the Caribbean and set out for Angola. Followed by United States warships, which kept him in sight without molesting him, Galvão could sail only to Recife, Brazil, where he turned the ship over to the authorities.[9]

The year 1961 saw also the seizure by Nehru's India of the Portuguese possessions there, after fruitless negotiations. The world seemed, in general, to side with India, although the world knew next to nothing of the history involved. Portugal had held Goa since 1510, at which time no Indian state existed or had been remotely dreamed of. Some Goans were Christians; their business associations abroad had been mostly with Portuguese Mozambique, and there is no evidence that a majority of them wished to change their status. Portugal grieved over the loss but could do nothing; it would have been wise to have anticipated events and ceded Goa and the other coastal possessions to India years earlier.

Meanwhile, António de Fragoso Carmona, President of Portugal, had died in 1951 at the age of eighty-two. He had been elected again in 1949, not altogether without opposition, and his death created more complications for Salazar than the world generally supposed. Obituaries described Carmona as a colorless figurehead, which was no adequate description of a man who had been his country's ablest general, had deposed Gomes da Costa, had ruled the nation for several years, and had installed Salazar in power. The old president commanded considerable prestige to the day of his death, and his passing raised a new problem. Should Salazar, as some urged, assume the national presidency himself and combine the executive powers under his own name? He declined to do so, and arranged for the election of Francisco Craveiro Lopes, from all evidence a rather uninteresting figure.

9. Galvão's own book describing these events is entitled *Santa Maria: My Crusade for Portugal*. For a recent survey of Portugal's colonial problems, see David M. Abshire and Michael A. Samuels, *Portuguese Africa*.

When the Lopes term expired in 1958, Portugal seemed on the verge of its first genuine presidential election in many years. The choice of the administration was Admiral Américo Tomás (b. 1894), but the opposition nominated General Humberto Delgado, who gave promise of waging a vigorous campaign. The general pointed out serious weaknesses in the Portuguese economy and deplored the low national standard of living. If chosen president, his constitutional powers would permit him to dismiss Salazar, and he announced that he would do so. He evidently realized that he would never be allowed to win by constitutional means and therefore planned to resort to armed revolution. "Unfortunately," he later wrote, "the officers taking part refused at the last moment to go forward in this patriotic venture."

Some sort of election was held in 1958, and Admiral Tomás proved the winner, though not until Delgado had demonstrated considerable strength and given evidence of popularity. It was probably fortunate for Portugal that this general was defeated, as he seemed to have only a negative program and demonstrated no understanding of the genuine needs of the country. Furthermore, he was a rather vain, blustering person who commanded little respect among thoughtful Portuguese and was not the man to give his nation respect abroad. He ultimately went to Brazil and after he returned to Europe, was found murdered in Spanish territory near Badajoz.

The Delgado campaign for the presidency had given the Salazar administration enough of a scare to cause it to amend the election clause of the constitution. By an amendment of 1959, it was ruled that henceforth the president should be chosen by an electoral college instead of by popular referendum. This understandably made the situation easier to control, and it permitted Admiral Tomás to be chosen again, this time easily, in 1965.

THE NEW REGIME

Salazar governed Portugal until September 6, 1968, when he suffered a massive stroke that terminated his active career. Portugal and the world waited for several days while doctors ascertained that no recovery was possible. The main supporters of the dictator grieved and feared a revolution, but nothing out of the way happened and Portuguese life went on as usual. The press of the world prepared

obituaries, but these proved somewhat premature, as the aged statesman did not die until July 1970, when a more or less grateful nation
awarded him a magnificent funeral.

The stroke placed President Tomás in an unprecedented position; his hitherto theoretical power to appoint the head of the council
now became a reality. A successor must be named at once, and the
president seems to have hesitated between several possible candidates
until he decided on Professor Marcello Caetano (b. 1906), who had
once worked closely with Salazar, though their relations had recently
been more distant.

Caetano, at his induction into office, spoke modestly, saying that
he would continue his illustrious predecessor's basic policies but make
some changes. He likened himself to a pupil following in the foot-
steps of a revered teacher but stated that it would be a mistake for a
pupil merely to emulate his predecessor.[10]

The new head of the council was a graduate of Lisbon University,
with a degree in law. At an early age he had held office under Salazar
and was one of those instrumental in drawing up the Constitution
of 1933, whose leading theoretician he had been. Caetano later became Rector of Lisbon University, but resigned, though continuing as
a professor of law, in 1962 when police invaded its precincts without
his permission and injured several people.

Caetano's taking of office brought about some liberalization of
Portugal. The press became freer and able to criticize the government,
which it was even encouraged to do. Periodically the censors, hold-
overs from Salazar days, displayed their old tendencies, but such
reversion was spasmodic and grew rarer as time passed. However,
editors and public alike were so conditioned by the enforced silence
of the last forty years that the former sometimes censored news needlessly and from force of habit. One aspect of the old censorship remained; it was still dangerous to antagonize a powerful member of
the government.

Social legislation, some of it "placed on the statute books as
window dressing" by Salazar, began at last to be implemented. Wages
increased and a much more cheerful tone emanated from the working
class, although the workers' condition remained bad. There was still
much absentee landlordism in Portugal, with the average proprietor

10. There is a short life history of Caetano in *Current Biography Yearbook*,
1970.

showing little social conscience. As a result, clandestine emigration by the peasants still went on. It remained inadvisable for them to go to Spain, for there, if caught and identified, they would be returned to Portugal by the authoritarian state. Because the peasants were "not safe until they crossed the Pyrenees," it was still best for them to escape by water if possible.

The University of Coimbra furnished a case illustrating the new Portugal; unsure of itself and with no definite bearings. The university became more liberal than under Salazar, yet some of the old restrictions continued—students might not hold meetings without official permission, for to do so remained a legal offense. In other ways more latitude was allowed, but the Coimbra students, not having tasted even limited freedom for many academic generations, seemed puzzled and uncertain of what to do with it. Despite the law, some general protest meetings took place, but these were described as pathetic and ineffectual. The students seemed favorable to Caetano and appeared to consider him their friend, for they remembered his resignation as Rector at Lisbon after the police raid. They had no wish to embarrass him, and their feeling of freedom meanwhile grew, if only gradually.

Salazar and Caetano, though both Portuguese with some characteristics in common, were otherwise of entirely different backgrounds. Salazar, a lifelong celibate trained for the priesthood, lived the life of a monk. Caetano, a professor of law and very much a family man, had never been so remote from the world as had his famous predecessor; he was "humanized" by his daily living and contacts with other people. He showed awareness of the economic paralysis that Salazar's tight policies imposed on Portugal and made a beginning of thawing out the nation's commerce, industry, and banking system. This, and higher wages, meant some price inflation, although the government managed to keep costs under fair control.

The arrival of Caetano on the national scene clearly meant some diminution of Church influence in national life. This had always been somewhat exaggerated in foreign minds, principally because of Salazar himself, under whom the Church, though not formally reestablished, was to all intents and purposes established. Recent Church appointments have shown more liberal and relaxed tendencies than in the past.

Finally, communism seemed no nearer to gaining popularity in Portugal than before, although a few Marxists have been in evidence who have nevertheless had no apparent impact upon popular thought.

Portugal can never forget Salazar, and a recent statement to the effect that the old man is today nearly forgotten is manifestly untrue. A nation can scarcely forget someone who only recently dominated every feature of its life for four decades. But, although there can be favorable judgments of him in many matters, it was more than time for him to go.

Suggested Readings

This bibliography favors writings in English to the extent possible. The modern historiography of Portugal begins with Alexandre Herculano de Carvalho e Araujo's *História de Portugal desde o Começo da Monarchia até o Fim do Reinado de Affonso III*, originally 4 vol. (1846–1853), but this is suggested only for those specializing in Portuguese history. More recent multivolume works are by Damião Peres et al., *História de Portugal. Edição Monumental*, 8 vol. (Barcelos, 1928–1937) and Fortunato de Almeida, *História de Portugal*, 6 vol. (Coimbra, 1922–1929).

Other writings covering long periods are by Hernani Cidade et al., *Os Grandes Portugueses*, 2 vol. (Lisbon, 1961), uneven in quality; and António José Saraiva et al., *História da Cultura em Portugal*, 3 vol. (Lisbon, 1950–1962), solid but extending only to the late sixteenth century.

One-volume works include José Ameal's *História de Portugal* (Oporto, 1940), too conservative for many modern tastes; and two works by H. V. Livermore: *A History of Portugal* (Cambridge, England, 1947), and *A New History of Portugal* (Cambridge, England, 1966). More brief is Charles E. Nowell's *A History of Portugal* (New York, 1952).

Prehistoric and Roman Portugal are covered differently by Dan Stanislawski, in *The Individuality of Portugal* (Austin, 1959), and Paul MacKendrick, *The Iberian Stones Speak: Archaeology in Spain and Portugal* (New York, 1969), Stanislawski concentrating on geography and MacKendrick on artifacts. Arab conquest and early rule in Iberia is covered by E. Levi-Provençal, *España Musulmana hasta la Caida del*

Califato de Córdoba, 711–1031, trans. from the French by Emilio Garcia Gómez (Madrid, 1950).

Portuguese national beginnings are described by Tomaz da Fonseca, D. *Afonso Henriques e a Fundação da Nacionalidade Portuguesa* (Coimbra, 1949), a documented study of the founder of the monarchy. The medieval history of Portugal, covered in the general works cited, is also partly covered in the interesting book by Bailey W. Diffie, *Prelude to Empire: Portugal Overseas before Henry the Navigator* (Lincoln, Nebr., 1960). Social history is furnished by A. H. de Oliveira Marques, *Daily Life in Portugal in the Late Middle Ages,* trans. S. S. Wyatt (Madison, Milwaukee, and London, 1971). Commercial beginnings are described by Charles Verlinden, *The Beginnings of Modern Colonization: Eleven Essays with an Introduction,* trans. Yvonne Freccero (Ithaca, 1970).

Peter Edward Russell's *The English Intervention in Spain and Portugal in the Time of Edward III and Richard II* (Oxford, 1955) describes the Battle of Aljubarrota and the accession of John of Avís. Francis M. Rogers provides what amounts to a biography of Prince Pedro, with much material concerning Henry, in *The Travels of the Infante Dom Pedro of Portugal* (Cambridge, Mass., 1961). Vitorino Magalhães Godinho, in *A Economia dos Descobrimentos Henriquinos* (Lisbon, 1962), covers the economic and much of the personal side of the prince-navigator's career. The source for Covilhã's travels is furnished by Francisco Álvares' *The Prester John of the Indies,* ed. C. F. Beckingham and G. W. B. Huntingford, 2 vol. (Cambridge, England, 1961), published in Portuguese in 1540. Edgar Prestage, in *The Portuguese Pioneers* (London, 1933), surveys Portuguese oceanic discovery to the sixteenth century. The edition of João de Barros used here is that prepared by António Baião (Coimbra, 1932). Elaine Sanceau's *The Perfect Prince: A Biography of the King Dom João II* (Barcelos, 1959) is the only life of John in English. The last Avís queen, accused of poisoning her husband, is studied, as far as possible, by João Ameal, in *Dona Leonor, "Princeza Perfeitissima"* (Oporto, 1943). Charles Ralph Boxer's *The Portuguese Seaborne Empire, 1415–1825* (New York, 1969) covers Portuguese imperialism from Avís times.

The Beja period is emphasized in all the general histories. Vasco da Gama's voyage to India and back is described by a participant, probably Álvaro Velho, in *Roteiro da Primeira Viagem de Vasco da Gama,* ed. A. Fontoura da Costa (Lisbon, 1960). A readable life of Gama himself is by Henry H. Hart, *Sea Road to the Indies* (New York, 1950).

The movement called Sebastianism and its resultant pretenders is described by Mary Elizabeth Brooks in *A King for Portugal* (Madison and Milwaukee, 1964). The territorial losses of Portugal in the Spanish period are explained by Charles Ralph Boxer, *The Dutch Seaborne Empire, 1600–1800* (New York, 1965). Partly on the same theme is Boxer's *The Dutch in Brazil, 1624–1654* (Oxford, 1957). Underlying economic causes of the Portuguese revolt from Spain in 1640 are furnished by Vitorino Magalhães Godinho, *Ensaios* (Lisbon, 1968), vol. II. The Methuen Treaty is explained by Alan David Francis in his *The Methuens and Portugal, 1691–1708* (Cambridge, England, 1966). Much of interest regarding the treaty is furnished by Armando Marques Guedes, in *A Aliança Inglêsa* (*Notas de História Diplomática*) *1383–1943* (Lisbon, 1943). Harold Edward Stephen Fisher, in *The Portugal Trade: A Study of Anglo-Portuguese Commerce, 1700–1770* (London, 1971), explains many aftereffects of the treaty. Henry Kamen's *The War of Succession in Spain, 1700–15* (Bloomington, London, 1969) is primarily concerned with Spain, but does survey Portugal's part in the war.

The only biographer of Pombal in English is Sir Marcus Cheke's entertaining *Dictator of Portugal: A Life of the Marquis of Pombal, 1699–1782* (London, 1938; Freeport, N.Y., 1969). The economic side of the dictator's administration is analyzed by Jorge Borges de Macedo in *A Situação Económica no Tempo de Pombal* (Oporto, 1951). The great earthquake and its consequences are well described by T. D. Kendrick, *The Lisbon Earthquake* (London, 1951). Cheke's *Carlota Joaquina, Queen of Portugal* (London, 1947) furnishes interesting sidelights regarding Portuguese life in the late eighteenth century.

Effects of the French Revolution and the Peninsular War are covered in the general histories of Portugal. For Wellington's part, Elizabeth Longford's *Wellington: The Years of the Sword* (New York and Evanston, 1969) is entertaining and scholarly. Michael Glover's *Wellington's Peninsular Victories* (New York, 1963) contains good information about the Tôrres Vedras campaign.

The Bragança residence in Brazil is described in detail by Tobias Monteiro in his *História do Imperio: A Elaboração da Independencia* (Rio de Janeiro, 1927). The best account of the life of Emperor Pedro is Octavio Tarquinio de Sousa's *Vida de D. Pedro I*, 3 vol. (São Paulo, 1954). Manoel de Oliveira Lima furnishes an account of Miguel in *D. Miguel no Trono, 1828–1833* (Coimbra, 1933).

Portuguese problems, mostly economic, in the early nineteenth century are discussed by Joel Serrão in *Temas Oitocentistas*, 2 vol. (Lisbon, 1959–1962). The career of Pedro V is covered in two works by Ruben Andresen Leitão: *Cartas de D. Pedro V aos seus Contemporâneos* (Lisbon, 1961), and *D. Pedro V—um Homen e um Rei* (Oporto, 1950).

James A. Duffy, in *Portuguese Africa* (Cambridge, Mass., 1959), surveys the subject from its beginning. R. J. Hammond's *Portugal and Africa, 1815–1910* (Stanford, 1966), and Eric Axelson's *Portugal and the Scramble for Africa, 1875–1891* (Johannesburg, 1967) are both primarily concerned with the partition, Hammond mainly from the European and Axelson from the African point of view. Marquês de Lavradio, in *Portugal em África depois de 1851* (Lisbon, 1936), summarizes Anglo-Portuguese relations and publishes important documents. Anglo-Portuguese rivalry in eastern Africa is covered by A. H. Hanna in *The Beginnings of Nyasaland and North-Eastern Rhodesia* (Oxford, 1956).

The encounter between Johnston and Serpa Pinto is described by Roland Oliver in *Sir Harry Johnston and the Scramble for Africa* (London, 1959). The attempt by Paiva Couceiro to make the *Côr-de-Rosa* plan a reality is documented by Norton de Mattos in *Angola. Ensaio sobre a Vida e Acção de Paiva Couceiro em Angola* (Lisbon, 1948).

The best account of the life of King Carlos is that of Francisco José Rocha Martins, *D. Carlos. História de seu Reinado* (privately printed, 1926). The war with Gungunhana is described by Eduardo de Noronha in his *Mousinho de Albuquerque: O Militar—O Colonial—O Administrador* (Lisbon, 1934), and by António Enes, *A Guerra de África em 1895* (Lisbon, 1898, 1945). The nearly contemporary situation in Africa is set forth by James Duffy in *Portugal in Africa* (Cambridge, Mass., 1962) and Ronald Chilcote, *Portuguese Africa* (Englewood Cliffs, N.J., 1967). Most contemporary is *Portuguese Africa: A Handbook*, ed. David M. Abshire and Michael A. Samuels (New York, Washington, and London, 1969).

A description of the republican revolution that is conservative in tone has been written by Jesús Pabón, *La República Portuguesa*, 2 vol. (Madrid, 1941–1945), and extends to the rise of Salazar. Vicente de Bragança-Cunha's *Revolutionary Portugal, 1910–1936* (London, 1937) contains shrewd and generally derogatory remarks about the republic and the early Salazar regime. The banknote fraud is described by Sir Cecil H. Kisch in *The Portuguese Bank Note Case: The Story and Solution of a Financial Perplexity* (London, 1932).

Works on Salazar generally include accounts of the overthrow of the republic by Gomes da Costa and Carmona. Of those dealing with the dictator, Christian Rudel's *Le Portugal et Salazar* (Paris, 1967) is unfavorable, whereas Jacques Ploncard d'Assac's *Salazar* (Paris, 1967) is laudatory. A third French writer, Christine Garnier, *Salazar in Portugal: An Intimate Portrait* (New York, 1954), adopted the different approach of interviewing Salazar and others, including Cardinal Cerejeira. The latest work on the subject, by Hugh Kay, *Salazar and Modern Portugal* (London, 1970), was completed after the crippling stroke laid Salazar low, and hence has a little to say about the following regime of Marcello Caetano. Kay is admirably balanced in his treatment of Salazar. Worth mentioning is the book by Henrique Galvão, *My Crusade for Portugal* (Cleveland and New York, 1961), which, because of the late Galvão's known views, is devastating to the Salazar regime.

Portuguese literature, in addition to the mentioned work by Saraiva, is dealt with by Aubrey F. G. Bell in *Portuguese Literature* (Oxford, 1922); Charles Ralph Boxer, in *Three Historians of Portuguese Asia:*

Barros, Couto, and Bocarro (Macao, 1947); Elizabeth Feist Hirsch, in *Damião de Gois: The Life and Thought of a Portuguese Humanist, 1502–1574* (The Hague, 1967); Henry H. Hart, *Luis de Camöens and the Epic of the Lusiads* (Norman, Okla., 1962); Fidelino de Figueiredo, *Literatura Portuguese* (Rio de Janeiro, 1940), and Clovis Ramalhete, *Eça de Queiróz* (São Paulo, 1943).

Index

175